LIFE IS SHORT...

MAKE THE REST OF YOUR LIFE THE BEST OF YOUR LIFE

Priceless Nuggets of Life-Changing
WISDOM
From Great Minds of the Past and Present

EARL RUNCAN

TRILOGY

Trilogy Christian Publishers

A Wholly Owned Subsidiary of Trinity Broadcasting Network

2442 Michelle Drive

Tustin, CA 92780

For information, address Trilogy Christian Publishing

Rights Department, 2442 Michelle Drive, Tustin, Ca 92780.

For information about special discounts for bulk purchases, please contact Trilogy Christian Publishing.

10 9 8 7 6 5 4 3 2 1

Library of Congress Cataloging-in-Publication Data is available.

ISBN 979-8-89333-400-5

ISBN 979-8-89333-401-2 (ebook)

ACKNOWLEDGMENTS

I am eternally thankful to all the individuals highlighted in this book and for their wisdom that has helped me grow personally and spiritually beyond all I could have ever imagined or hoped for.

Grateful and sincere thanks to my wife, our daughters, and their husbands for the fun and laughter we shared one beautiful sunny morning while vacationing at the beach. Breakfast included brainstorming ideas for the covers and titles of this book. It was truly a God-blessed family time together. Our four grandchildren and one of their friends were still sleeping off the previous day's ocean and pool activities! I love you all so much more than words can ever express.

Finally, to God alone be all glory, honor, and praise!

TABLE OF CONTENTS

INTRODUCTION

I am writing this "Introduction" both with great sadness as well as great joy in my heart! I am deeply saddened because a wonderful God-fearing friend and mentor of mine in years past died very unexpectedly. However, I am rejoicing in my heart because he is now at peace in his heavenly home. Brad (not his real name) will be greatly missed by all whose lives he touched in so many different and amazing ways.

Brad was a committed follower of Jesus Christ. He was a faithful and loving husband, father, and grandfather. He was very athletic, in great physical shape, a very successful business owner, and a sincere and generous friend to many folks from all walks of life.

I am sharing this with you because everyone who knew Brad was in utter shock at his passing. When I heard the news, all that kept running through my mind was, "Life is short, so make every day count, fulfilling the purposes God created you for." I would also say that if you don't believe in God, life is still short, so make every day count, working to accomplish all the things that are near and dear to your heart.

I have been blogging on Wisdom-Matters.com since 2017. I started blogging about the many experiences I've had as a business manager, entrepreneur, business owner, and as an elder in the Evangelical Presbyterian Church since 1991.

I share biblical wisdom, leadership wisdom, financial wisdom, wisdom relevant to current events, and wisdom for personal and spiritual growth from the many books I've read over the years. I also share wisdom from my personal experiences, and from the mentors and close friends who have poured into my life.

Paying it forward, if you will, so others can learn from my mistakes and possibly take away something positive from any successes I've had. More importantly, from the great success stories and wisdom of some great minds of the past and present, I look forward to introducing you to in this book.

One dictionary I use defines *wisdom* as "the ability to discern right choices, and the ability to make wise choices depends on the possession of relevant knowledge." The great theologian Charles Spurgeon put it this way: *"Wisdom is the right use of knowledge. To know is not to be wise. Many men know a great deal and are all the greater fools for it. But to know how to use knowledge is to have wisdom."*

If you, or others you know, are struggling right now with a lack of direction and purpose in life or just need a fresh reboot, consider this quote by author James R. Sherman: *"You can't go back and change the beginning, but you can start where you are and change the ending."*

Whether you are still in school, want to start a business, or want to climb the corporate ladder, I am confident that the wisdom in this book will prepare you to shine far above everyone else trying to beat you to the top utilizing their own wisdom and understanding.

In one easy-to-read book, you can start applying these priceless nuggets of wisdom to your life immediately and begin experiencing a new life filled with purpose, peace, and prosperity in whatever you choose to do with the days you have left on this earth.

You are about to embark on the journey of a lifetime by immersing yourself in all the WISDOM you'll ever need to achieve successful life transformation beyond your wildest hopes and dreams. A new life filled with purpose, peace, and prosperity.

I would highly recommend and encourage you to read this book at least once cover-to-cover. You can then decide where you want to focus your attention and begin putting these priceless nuggets of wisdom into ACTION.

READY => SET => LIFE IS SHORT =>
GO BE ALL YOU WERE CREATED TO BE

Before we get started on the serious stuff, I'd like to share a bit of humor with you to hopefully put a smile on your face as you prepare to become the "new you."

An English woman looking for a room in Switzerland asked the schoolmaster of the village where she wanted to live to help her. After finding a place that suited her, she returned to London for her baggage. Once there, however, she remembered that she hadn't asked about a bathroom, or "water closet," as she called it. So, she wrote the village schoolmaster with her question, referring to these facilities in her letter as a "WC."

The schoolmaster, puzzled by these initials, sought the help of a parish priest. The priest decided the woman must be asking about a Wayside Chapel.

You can imagine the woman's confusion when she received the following letter from the schoolmaster:

Dear Madam:

I regret very much the delay in answering your letter. But I now take pleasure in informing you that a "WC" is located about 9 miles from the house, in the center of a beautiful grove of trees. It is capable of seating 250 people at a time. It is open Tuesday, Thursday, and Sunday each week. I admit it is quite a distance away if you are in the habit of going regularly, but no doubt you will be pleased to know that a great number of people take their lunches along and make a day of it. They usually arrive early and stay late.

The last time my wife and I went was six years ago. It was so crowded we had to stand the whole time we were there. It may interest you to know that there is a supper being planned to raise money to buy more seats. Likewise, it may interest you to know that my daughter met her husband for the first time in the "WC," and they were later married in the "WC."

I would like to say it pains me very much not to be able to go more regularly, but it is surely no lack of desire on my part. As we grow older, it seems to be more of an effort, particularly in cold weather. If you should decide to come for a visit, perhaps I could go with you the first time you go, sit with you, and introduce you to all the other folks. Remember, this is a friendly community.

Yours truly,

The Schoolmaster

PROLOGUE: Wisdom for Starting Each Day

I drafted these nuggets of wisdom below in December 2018 to share with our amazing and talented grandchildren. I put a copy in each of their Christmas stockings and encouraged them to read the one corresponding to each day of the week. It wasn't a very exciting stocking stuffer, I know! My hope and prayers are they will take this wisdom with them, apply it to their lives daily as they grow, and even share it with their friends.

It didn't take long to realize these nuggets of wisdom might also be beneficial for anyone desiring to make positive changes in their lives, no matter their age.

I can't think of a better way to start each week than by reading and meditating on these daily nuggets of wisdom and committing to live by them. I believe the world would be a far better place if each of us just started here!

Full Disclosure: Each of the daily quotes below is from sources other than my own, so I cannot take credit for originating them. However, I did add some content to each.

Monday: *Job security is your ability to produce. Never stop learning and giving your very best effort every day.*

Tuesday: *Hard work beats talent when talent fails to work hard. Don't take your God-given talents and abilities for granted. No pain, no gain!*

Wednesday: *Moral & ethical <u>character</u> is the will to do what is right, as God defines right in the Holy Bible, regardless of personal cost. Sometimes, doing the right thing hurts!*

Thursday: *What's popular is not always right, and what's right is not always popular. One bad decision can lead to a lifetime of regrets!*

Friday: *You can never be at the right place, at the right time, doing the right thing if you're with the wrong crowd! Show me your friends, and I'll show you your future.*

Saturday: *Run from evil and hold onto what is good. Sin has consequences!*

Even if you don't believe in the power of prayer, you can't go wrong making the "Sunday Prayer" below your very own every day of the week, let alone on Sundays.

It's a prayer written by General Douglas MacArthur to his only son during World War II. I've reworded it a bit to personalize it.

Sunday: *O Lord, make me strong enough to know when I am weak and brave enough to face myself when I am afraid; one who will be proud and unbending in honest defeat and humble and gentle in victory.*

Make me a person whose wishes will not take the place of good deeds, who will know You, and that to know myself is the foundation stone of knowledge.

Lead me, I pray, not in the path of ease and comfort, but under the stress and spur of difficulties and challenges. Here, let me learn to stand up in the storm; here, let me learn compassion for those who fail.

Make me a person whose heart will be clear, whose goal will be high, who will master myself before I seek to master others, one who will reach into the future, yet never forget the past.

And after all these things are mine, O Lord, add, I pray, enough of a sense of humor, so that I may always be serious, yet never take myself too seriously. Give me humility so that I may always remember the simplicity of true greatness, the open mind of true wisdom, and the weakness of true strength.

Then, O Lord, I will dare to whisper, I have not lived in vain.

Parents and grandparents, please bless your children and grandchildren with a copy of this Daily Wisdom. Encourage them to use it as a moral compass as they grow and navigate through this crazy, ever-changing world we live in.

PART 1:
Personal Growth & Leadership Wisdom

CHAPTER 1:
Attitude Is Everything

I've heard it said we are given a menu of two choices when we wake up to face each new day: a good attitude or a bad attitude. It's our choice, and ultimately, our daily choices will lead to lives filled with joy and success or lives filled with frustration and failure.

When someone tells you, "It Can't Be Done," REMEMBER; those are their limits, not yours. —Author Unknown

John Maxwell's book, *The Winning Attitude*, is a tremendous resource for encouragement and understanding why our attitude is such an important part of who we are and who we will become.

Why Our Attitude is So Important

John Maxwell writes, "The attitude is an inward feeling expressed by behavior. That is why an attitude can be seen without a word being said. Of all the things we wear, our expression is the most important. Since an attitude often is expressed by our body language and by the looks on our faces, it can be contagious."

Maxwell says, "Sooner or later, what is happening within us will affect what is happening without. A hardened attitude is a dreaded disease. It causes a closed mind and a dark future. When the attitude is positive and conducive to growth, the mind expands, and the progress begins."

Maxwell asks, "What is an attitude?

- It is the 'advance man' of our true selves.
- Its roots are inward, but its fruits are outward.
- It is our best friend or our worst enemy.
- It is more honest and more consistent than our words.

- It is an outward look based on past experiences.
- It is a thing that draws people to us or repels them.
- It is never content until it is expressed.
- It is the librarian of our past.
- It is the speaker of our present.
- It is the prophet of our future."

Maxwell goes on to say, "We live in a world of words. Attached to these words are meanings that bring varied responses from us. Words such as *happiness*, *acceptance*, *peace*, and *success* describe what each of us desires. But there is one word that will either heighten the possibility of our desires being fulfilled or prevent them from becoming a reality within us. *Attitude.*"

Maxwell believes, "Our attitude is the primary force that will determine whether we succeed or fail. For some, attitude presents a difficulty in every opportunity; for others, it presents an opportunity in every difficulty. Some climb with a positive attitude, while others fall with a negative perspective. The very fact that the attitude 'makes some' while 'breaking others' is significant enough for us to explore its importance."

To explore the importance of *attitude*, Maxwell offers seven Attitude Axioms:

"*Attitude Axiom #1: Our attitude determines our approach to life.* Our attitude tells us what we expect from life. If our 'nose' is pointed up, we are taking off; if it is pointed down, we may be headed for a crash.

Adopting a good, healthy attitude toward life does not affect society nearly as much as it affects us. The change cannot come from others. It must come from us. We are individually responsible for our view of life.

Attitude Axiom #2: Our attitude determines our relationships with people. Observe the difference between executives defined as 'high achievers' (those who generally have a healthy attitude) and 'low achievers' (those who generally have an unhealthy attitude):

- High achievers tended to care about people as well as profits; low achievers were preoccupied with their own security.
- High achievers viewed subordinates optimistically; low achievers showed a basic distrust of subordinates' abilities.
- High achievers sought advice from their subordinates; low achievers didn't.
- High achievers were listeners; low achievers avoided communication and relied on policy manuals.

A negative past experience sometimes paralyzes our thinking and our attitude.

Attitude Axiom #3: Often, our attitude is the only difference between success and failure. History's greatest achievements have been made by men who excelled only slightly over the masses of others in their fields.

Attitude Axiom #4: Our attitude at the beginning of a task will affect its outcome more than anything else. Many times, we have been guilty of viewing our future challenges as the sunset of life rather than the sunrise of a bright new opportunity.

Attitude Axiom #5: Our attitude can turn our problems into blessings. When confronted with a difficult situation, a person with an outstanding attitude makes the best of it while he gets the worst of it. Life can be likened to a grindstone. Whether it grinds you down or polishes you depends upon what you are made of.

Attitude Axiom #6: Our attitude can give us an uncommonly positive perspective. The individual whose attitude causes him to approach life from an entirely positive perspective is not always understood. He is what some would call a 'no-limit person.' In other words, he doesn't accept the normal limitations of life like most people. He is unwilling to accept 'the accepted' just because it is accepted. His response to self-limiting conditions will probably be 'Why?' instead of an 'Okay.' He has limitations in his life. His gifts are not so plentiful that he cannot fail. But he is determined to walk to the very edge of his potential or the potential of a project before he accepts defeat.

Attitude Axiom #7: Our attitude is not automatically good just because we may be Christian. It is noteworthy that the seven deadly sins (pride, covetousness, lust, envy, anger, gluttony, and sloth) are all matters of attitude, inner spirit, and motives.

Christians who possess no greater cause than themselves are not as happy as those who do not know Christ as Savior yet have a purpose greater than themselves."

CHAPTER 2: What It Takes to Be a Winner

Deep down, we all want to win at whatever we are doing in life. Excerpts from *The Winners Manual* written by coach Jim Tressel during his tenure as head coach of The Ohio State Buckeyes football team can put us on track for becoming a winner no matter what we do in life and no matter what life throws our way.

Winners see the dreams and develop plans, while losers see the obstacles and develop excuses. —Coach Lisle

Coach Tressel has identified ten fundamentals essential for winners. We'll briefly review each fundamental and the resources coach Tressel has used to shape his character as well as his coaching staff and, most importantly, his players.

#1—ATTITUDE

The greatest discovery of my generation is that human beings can alter their lives by altering their attitudes of mind. —William James

Coach Tressel says, "We have to understand that our thinking affects everything we do. A good attitude can overcome some other limitations, but even great talent can't overcome the wrong attitude."

Two things define you. Your patience when you have nothing, and your attitude when you have everything. —Author Unknown

Paradise is where I am. —Voltaire

Coach T. reminds us, "If you're in paradise where you are—not wishing you were someplace else—that's the right attitude. If you're always wishing you were someplace else, what you'll discover is that the other place has just as many problems and difficulties—maybe more—as the place where you are right now."

The empires of the future are the empires of the mind. —Winston Churchhill

Coach T. says, "Attitude is not something that comes by instinct. It has to be practiced over and over or relearned over and over. We have to choose to have a good attitude."

Coach Tressel also believes there are three basic components to the right attitude—*Gratitude*, *Humility*, and *Enthusiasm.*

Gratitude

It is impossible to be grateful and unhappy at the same time. —Author Unknown

"PROMISE YOURSELF…

- To be so strong that nothing can disturb your peace of mind
- To look at the sunny side of everything and make your optimism come true
- To think only of the best
- To be just as enthusiastic about the success of others as you are about your own
- To forget the mistakes of the past and press on to the greater achievements of the future
- To share the greater achievements of the future
- To give so much time to the improvement of yourself that you have no time to criticize others
- To be too large for worry, too strong for fear, and too happy to permit the presence of trouble."

If you see no reason for giving thanks, the fault lies within yourself. —Tecumseh

Humility

If we were humble, nothing would change us—neither praise nor discouragement. —Mother Teresa

Humility precedes honor. —Proverbs 18:12 (NLT)

Graveyards are full of irreplaceable men. —Charles De Gaulle

With humility comes wisdom. —Proverbs 11:2 (NLT)

Enthusiasm

Flaming enthusiasm, backed by horse sense and persistence, is the quality that most frequently makes for success. —Dale Carnegie

None are so old as those who have outlived enthusiasm. —Henry David Thoreau

You may have heard this one before, but it's worth repeating.

There are three types of people:

1. Those who make things happen;
2. Those who watch things happen;
3. And those who say, "What happened?"

Which one are you?

#2—DISCIPLINE

It is not enough to get things done; they must be done right. —Arthur T. Hadley

Those who work the hardest, who subject themselves to the strictest discipline, who give up certain pleasurable things in order to achieve a goal, are the happiest. —Brutus Hamilton, Olympic Decathlete and Coach

Start by doing what's necessary, then what's possible,

and suddenly you are doing the impossible. —Saint Francis of Assisi

Coach Tressel states, "In today's culture, *discipline* is considered a negative, almost a foul word.

We associate discipline with a strict, narrow lifestyle in which we're punished if we're not obedient. We tend to think that a disciplined life is restrictive and controlled by some outside authority figure with a sour disposition. In short, we think that a life of discipline means no freedom, no fun, and no joy. But nothing could be further from the truth. The fundamentals of discipline will actually help us live more freeing, invigorating lives."

Improving yourself is the best way to help your team. —Jim Tressel

A champion pays an extra price to be better than anyone else. —Paul "Bear" Bryant

Only a fool despises...discipline; whoever learns from correction is wise. —Proverbs 15:5 (NLT)

"WHEN NO ONE ELSE IS LOOKING—Discipline is what you do when no one else is looking! It's being considerate of the other person. Having good personal habits—you are polite, on time, and take care of business with pride. We must be disciplined as individuals first and then as a team."

Self-discipline is when you tell yourself to do something, and you don't talk back. —W. K. Hope

"A DISCIPLINED PLAYER…

1. Knows the importance of being on time.
2. Has learned the value of regular hours and good training habits from working hard in practice.
3. Has learned that the team comes before himself. This strengthens his character as he is sometimes called upon to sacrifice for others.

4. Has learned to take orders; in taking orders, he learns how to give them.
5. Knows that discipline is the essence of every successful organization; as a member of the team, he understands the need for it.
6. Has learned that many of these things establish a degree of self-discipline."

You have to have confidence in your ability and then be tough enough to follow through. —Rosalynn Carter

It was character that got us out of bed, commitment that moved us into action, and discipline that enabled us to follow through. —Zig Ziglar

Focus

Coach Tressel believes, "Focus is an important component of discipline. Focus is a critical part of discipline because there are many things going on around us that can draw us away from the singleness of thought we need to accomplish whatever the moment calls for.

- Focus is when your mental attention is centered on what you need to do. Nothing else can get into your head.
- Focus is when someone can resist temptation in the present to further pursue a goal in the future.
- Focus means concentrating on your responsibility.
- Focus means total concentration. Committing to something and staying with it until it is done and done right. Never giving up.
- Focus is the ability to concentrate on something by ignoring outside important forces that can interfere with the task at hand. Taking advantage of all opportunities that facilitate the task and increase the chance of success.

- Focus is disciplined and zeroed in on the goal and only the goal."

Now is everything you have to work with. When you live it fully, it is more than enough. —Ralph Marston

Obstacles are those frightful things you see when you take your eyes off the goal. —Hannah More (1745–1833)

Success is when you beat your fear of failing —Author Unknown

The man who succeeds above his fellows is the one who, early in life, clearly discerns his objective and, towards that objective, habitually directs his power. —Earl Nightingale

Coach Tressel sums up the topic of *focus* perfectly by reminding us, "You can tell that you're not focused when your brain and your rear end are in two different places."

#3—EXCELLENCE

The quality of a person's life is in direct proportion to their commitment to excellence, regardless of their chosen field of endeavor. —Vince Lombardi

Excellence is not an act...but a habit. —Aristotle

Risk more than others think is safe. Care more than others think is wise. Dream more than others think is practical. Expect more than others think is possible. —Cadet Maxim, U.S. Military Academy

It isn't hard to be good from time to time in sports. What's tough is being good every day. —Willie Mays (I believe this quote by Willie applies to life in general as well.)

Only those who have the patience to do simple things perfectly will acquire the skills to do difficult things easily. —Jim Tressel

The foundation of excellence lies in self-control. —H. L. Baugher

Quality is never an accident. It is always the result of intelligent effort. —John Ruskin

If you can't win, make the fellow ahead of you break the record. —Author Unknown

I can accept failure. Everyone fails at something. But I can't accept not trying. —Michael Jordan

The hallmark of excellence, the test of greatness, is consistency. —Jim Tressel

"YOU ARE AT THE TOP WHEN…

1. You have made friends with your past, and you are focused on the present and optimistic about the future.
2. You have the love of friends and the respect of your enemies.
3. You are filled with faith, hope, and love, and you live without anger, greed, guilt, envy, or thoughts of revenge.
4. You know that failure to stand for what is morally right is the prelude to being the victim of what is criminally wrong.
5. You are mature enough to delay gratification and shift your focus from your rights to your responsibilities.
6. You love the unlovable, give hope to the hopeless, friendship to the friendless, and encouragement to the discouraged.
7. You know that success (a win) doesn't make you and that failure (a loss) doesn't break you.
8. You can look back in forgiveness, forward in hope, down in compassion, and up with gratitude.
9. You are secure in who you are, so you are at peace with God and in fellowship with humanity.

10. You clearly understand that yesterday ended last night, that today is a brand-new day, and it is yours!
11. You know that "he who would be the greatest among you must become the servant of all."
12. You are pleasant to the grouchy, courteous to the rude, and generous to the needy because you know that the long-term benefits of giving and forgiving far outweigh the short-term benefits of receiving.
13. You recognize, confess, develop, and use your God-given physical, mental, and spiritual abilities to the glory of God and for the benefit of humankind.
14. You stand in front of the Creator of the universe, and He says to you, "Well done, my good and faithful servant."

If you heed your fears, you'll die, never knowing what a great person you might have been. —Dr. Robert Schuller

Coach Tressell concludes his discussion on this fundamental by encouraging us to "Use whatever duty you've been assigned today to exemplify excellence and see what that does for your own peace of mind as well as for the good of your team."

#4—FAITH & BELIEF

Faith doesn't mean the absence of fear. It means having the energy to go ahead, right alongside the fear. —Sharon Salzberg

Now faith is confidence in what we hope for and assurance about what we do not see. —Hebrews 11:1 (NIV)

Coach Tressel states, "There are two components to the fundamental of faith and belief: (1) the faith people have in something bigger than themselves and (2) the belief they have in themselves and what they're doing. Faith is who you are. Belief is what you do with your faith."

Champions believe in themselves even if no one else does. —Author Unknown

I think when you move past your fear and you go after your dreams wholeheartedly, you become free ... Move past the fear. —L L Cool J

The future belongs to those who believe in the beauty of their dreams. —Eleanor Roosevelt

To disbelieve is easy; to scoff is simple; to have faith is harder. —Louis L'Amour

Coach Tressel says, "Belief is centered more in the individual, and it represents a strong, internal feeling that suggests, 'I can do this.' At its core is the ability to move forward because of the evidence the person can see. He or she says, 'I believe in the people I'm with; I believe in the preparation I've made; I believe in the plan that's in place.'"

We are only beaten when we cease to believe what we can be. —Author Unknown

Nobody will believe in you unless you believe in yourself. —Liberace

There can be no progress if people have no faith in tomorrow. —John F. Kennedy

All I have seen teaches me to trust the Creator for all I have not seen. —Ralph Waldo Emerson

This poem by Walter D. Wintle says a lot about the component of belief:

If you think you're beaten, you are; If you think you dare not, you don't. If you'd like to win but think you can't, It's almost a cinch you won't. If you think you'll lose, you're lost, for out in the world, we find success begins with a fellow's will; It's all in the state of mind.

Full many a race is lost ere ever a step is run, and many a coward fails ere ever his work's begun. Think big, and your

deeds will grow; Think small, and you'll fall behind. Think that you can, and you will; It's all in the state of mind.

If you think you're outclassed, you are. You've got to think high to rise. You've got to be sure of yourself before you can ever win a prize. Life's battles don't always go to the stronger or faster man, but sooner or later, the man who wins is the fellow who thinks he can. It's all in the state of mind!

Our doubts are traitors and make us lose the good we oft might win by fearing to attempt. —William Shakespeare, *Measure for Measure*

Coach Tressel ends this fundamental by encouraging us, "Regardless of what aspect of life you want to name, whether it's about your faith or your family or a work assignment, nothing worthwhile is going to happen unless you believe.

That's why when we present success as a journey, we talk about having a plan and dreams. And then we have to go to work on those plans and dreams, all the while handling adversity and success. The key to all that is belief. Belief that we can do the task. Belief that we *will* do the task. Active believing reinforces the other fundamentals and helps make us winners."

#5—WORK

Whenever you start—give it your best. The opportunities are there to be anything you want to be. But wanting to be someone isn't enough; dreaming about it isn't enough; thinking about it isn't enough. You've got to study for it, work for it, fight for it with all your heart and soul because nobody is going to hand it to you. —General Colin Powell

Success doesn't come to you... you go to it. —Marva Collins

Work willingly at whatever you do, as though you were working for the Lord rather than for people. —Colossians 3:23 (NLT)

Even if you're on the right track, you'll get run over it you just sit there. —Will Rogers

Coach Tressel reminds us, "It's important to understand that work is not who you are; it's what you do. Many people get that backward and think their lives are defined by what they accomplish or by what position they hold…No matter what endeavor you pursue in life, if you want to succeed, you're going to have to work at it.

Some guys with a lot of natural talent come into our program at Ohio State and are blown away by the amount of study football takes. These are guys who were always the best players in youth football and in high school, and some have leaned on their talent to make up for any deficiencies in their fundamentals or work ethic. At the collegiate level, and certainly at the professional level, you can't get away with that. It takes a lot of work, a lot of conditioning, lots of repetitions each day, and then building on the knowledge you've gained until you get to a certain level of proficiency. And after you get to that point, it takes even more work to stay there."

Whether in sports or in a work environment, the wisdom above applies equally as well. It takes hard work and "continuous improvement" to stay on top of our game!

Coaches and players can say anything they want, but if they don't back it up with performance and hard work, the talking doesn't mean a thing. —Michael Jordan

Stopping a piece of work just because it's hard, either emotionally or imaginatively, is a bad idea. Sometimes, you have to go on when you don't feel like it. —Stephen King

Success is the intersection where dreams and hard work meet. —Jim Tressel

Whatever you do, don't do it halfway. —Bob Beamon

Opportunity is missed by most people because it's dressed in overalls and looks like work. —Thomas Edison

Coach Tressel shares the following story told to the players the night before the most challenging day of preseason: the running test.

"Every morning in Africa, a gazelle wakes up. It knows it must run faster than the fastest lion, or it will be killed. Every morning, the lion wakes up. It knows it must outrun the slowest gazelle, or it will starve to death. It doesn't matter whether you are a lion or a gazelle. When the sun comes up, you'd better be running!"

Coach T. also says, "On the journey to success, after we've made all our preparations—the goals and blueprints and dreams—the next step is to work toward those goals. To do that, we need two qualities that are vital to our work: *persistence* and *toughness*."

Persistence

Nothing in this world can take the place of persistence. Talent will not; nothing is more common than unsuccessful men with talent. Genius will not; unrewarded genius is almost a proverb. Education alone will not; the world is full of educated failures. Persistence and determination alone are omnipotent (all-powerful). —Calvin Coolidge

Passion makes every detail important. —G. K. Chesterton

Coach T. reminds us that "Persistence is a quality possessed by people who want to achieve. If they have a passionate desire to succeed, the goal becomes much more important than the obstacles thrown in their way. They realize that a single event, failure, or circumstance does not define them."

Whatever you do, do it passionately. Failure is an event, not a person. Every obstacle presents an opportunity...IF you're looking for it. Relax! You only fail when you quit. —Jim Tressel

One man with courage makes a majority. —Andrew Jackson

You never plow a field by turning it over in your mind. —Irish Proverb

Toughness

Everyone has a plan until they are hit. —Evander Holyfield

Coach T. believes, "True toughness comes from courageous actions and applies to every aspect of the game of life. We have to be tough enough to make good decisions—decisions we know are right, even in situations where the right thing may not be the most popular choice. This type of toughness may very well be the hardest thing for young athletes today."

I would add the "type of toughness" Coach Tressel is referring to above may very well be the most complex kind of toughness for any person to practice these days, young or old. A wrong five-second decision can lead to a lifetime of regrets!

Coach T. goes on to say, "Often, the most difficult challenges in life are situations that we can't explain. When life really punches you in the gut, you find out how much toughness and courage you truly possess."

#6—HANDLING ADVERSITY & SUCCESS

I asked God for strength that I might achieve. I was made weak that I might learn humbly to obey. I asked for health that I might do great things. I was given infirmity that I might do better things. I asked for riches that I might be happy. I was given poverty, that I might be wise. I asked for power that I might have the praise of men. I was given weakness that I might feel the need for God. I asked for all things that I might enjoy life.

I was given life that I might enjoy all things. I got nothing I asked for—but everything I had hoped for. Almost despite myself, my unspoken prayers were answered. I am, among men, most richly blessed!—Author Unknown (often attributed to an unknown Confederate soldier)

With champions, success is never unexpected; it's a natural result that comes from continuous, unselfish, unrelenting determination to win, never letting down, never letting outside influences into the game. —Harvey Mackay

Dear brothers and sisters, when troubles of any kind come your way, consider it an opportunity for great joy. For you know that when your faith is tested, your endurance has a chance to grow. So let it grow, for when your endurance is fully developed, you will be perfect and complete, needing nothing. —James 1:2–4 (NLT)

Great character is the cumulative result when great pain and great disappointment intersect in a man (or woman) *with a teachable spirit.* —Jim Tressel

Coach Tressel explains, "Adversity comes to us all—it's only a matter of when. The real question is not *whether* we'll face adversity but *how* we will respond to it when it comes. If our attitude is one that embraces learning and growing, we'll treat adversity as a stepping-stone to the success we desire rather than see it as an insurmountable obstacle. But if we have a negative attitude and become defensive at the first hint of criticism or begin to blame others for our mistakes, we'll miss the opportunity to develop into the types of people we want to be."

Our greatest glory is not in never failing, but in rising every time we fall. —Confucius.

There is no education like adversity. —Benjamin Disraeli

Success is a lousy teacher. It makes smart people think they can't lose. —Bill Gates

Coach T. says, "Success does things to you that adversity doesn't. It adds more things to your plate...But for everything that success adds to your schedule, it takes something else away.

Whether it's from your exercise time, your spiritual time, your family time, or your students' academic time, success takes away time and can distract you from your goals and plans.

It's interesting that adversity has the opposite effect. When you meet with adversity, you can often find yourself alone...No one's interested in your opinion about success. You don't have people clamoring for your time, so you have more time to yourself.

My point is that whether you have success or failure, you have a challenge ahead of you...You have to adjust whether the ball bounces your way or not. Everything that happens during the course of your journey is part of life, and you have to adjust."

There is no strength where there is no struggle. —Jim Tressel

Coach T. goes on to remind us, "Sometimes, even if we believe our steps are ordered, we don't see a purpose in the pain we're going through at the moment...In every phase of life, you're going to face opposition.

In every phase of life...there will be good pressure and bad pressures on your life. You have to learn how to handle those and respond well. If you're aware of the pressures, if you're *present* and are able to think through what you did wrong (identify), you can also figure out how to do it right (improve) and then practice the right steps to improve (implement). If you follow this three-step process—identify, improve, and implement—you'll not only 'cope' with adversity, but you'll also move forward stronger and with more passion toward your goals."

Face adversity promptly and without flinching, and you will reduce its impact. Never run from anything, and never quit. —Winston Churchill

In attacking adversity, only a positive attitude, alertness, and regrouping to basics can launch a comeback. —Pat Riley

The toughest thing about being a success is that you've got to keep being a success. —Irving Berlin

Coach Tressel ends this fundamental by admitting, "I have learned more from losses than I've ever learned from wins, but you can learn good life lessons from both. Don't let adversity or success derail your goals and dreams. Let them propel you forward."

#7—LOVE

You can give without loving, but you cannot love without giving. —Amy Carmichael

Life's most persistent and urgent question is: what are you doing for others?—Martin Luther King Jr.

Concern for man and his fate must form the chief interest of all technical endeavors...Never forget that in the midst of your diagrams and equations. —Albert Einstein

Coach Tressel says, "If we focus solely on winning and set aside the loving care of individuals, we place our team and ourselves at a disadvantage...As human beings, we were not made only to achieve things.

True winners in the game of life will not look merely at goals and achievements. True winners who are part of a winning team will care more about the people beside them in the trenches than they will about the trophy at the end of the journey. True winners will have compassion for their teammates and desire the good of others as well as their own."

Love cures all people—both the ones who give it and the ones who receive it. —Dr. Karl Menninger

True love will find an outlet in service. —Billy Graham

Coach T. believes, "Commitment is the key to every relationship. Whatever team you're on, whether it's a marriage, a family, a work team, or a sports team, in order to achieve whatever goals you've set, you must be bound together by a love that exhibits itself in extreme commitment and the laying down of one's life for the common good.

The failure to commit ourselves is evident in so many aspects of our society. People want to be 'cool' rather than committed. They want to be esteemed and lifted up. But you can't focus on being cool if you want to be a champion. You have to be willing to cry. You have to be willing to love. You have to be willing to commit."

All I ask is that you play better than you are. —Doc Spurgeon

When you help someone up a hill, you get that much closer to the top yourself. —Author Unknown

The true measure of a man is how he treats someone who can do him absolutely no good. —Ann Landers

Coach T. reminds us, "Love is not something we can turn on and off at will; it has to be ingrained in our being. It's a vital ingredient in a winner's game plan. And, like every other fundamental, it has to be worked on every day. The people around us will know if what we're expressing is genuine or not. Love must be a lifestyle."

#8—RESPONSIBILITY

When in doubt, tell the truth. —Mark Twain

Even children are known by the way they act, whether their conduct is pure, and whether it is right. —Proverbs 20:11 (NLT)

Associate yourself with men of good quality if you esteem your own reputation, for 'tis better to be alone than in bad company. —George Washington

Coach Tressel states, "The definitions of right and wrong keep shifting, and the line is fluid. Many people have no objective standard for judging what 'right' is.

So, discussing what it means to 'do right,' working through it, and practicing it becomes a welcome discipline for our players. It helps them define their own terms of right and wrong."

I must say here that if I didn't know coach Tressel was a strong Christian man, I would have to totally disagree with his last sentence above, *"It helps them define their own terms of right and wrong."* However, I know that Coach T. takes every opportunity possible to share biblical principles with his staff and players.

In this case, once God's principles of right and wrong are presented to the players, they are free to accept or reject them. In my opinion, rejecting God's commands and principles for what is right and what is wrong is not a wise choice for anyone!

Coach T. says, "Nobody wants to be talked to like a child. But we know that, like children, young adults can forget about the importance of being responsible and doing right.

In one impetuous moment, they can lose all they've worked so hard to achieve. So we tell them, 'We know you already know this, but we want to remind you.' We want them to know how to distinguish wrong from right, bad from good, and better from best."

The reputation of a thousand years may be determined by the conduct of one hour. —Japanese Proverb.

There is no pillow so soft as a clear conscience. —French Proverb

Coach T. goes on to say, "I like to use the word *conscience* instead of *character* because it takes the focus off of our opinion and puts it on the actions of the other person. The book of Proverbs says, *'Fear of the LORD is the foundation of true knowledge, but fools despise wisdom and discipline'* (Proverbs 1:7, NLT). Reverence for God, a conscious desire not to disappoint Him, is where it all begins."

I firmly believe Coach Tressel would fully agree with Pastor Andy Stanley's definition of *character* and use it right along with Proverbs 1:7— *"Character is the will to do what is right, as God defines right, regardless of personal cost."*

Hold yourself to a higher standard than anyone expects of you. Never excuse yourself. —Henry Ward Beecher

There is a choice you have to make in everything you do. So keep in mind that in the end, the choice you make makes you. —John Wooden

Action springs not from thought but from a readiness for responsibility. —Dietrich Bonhoeffer.

Class

Manners are like the zero in arithmetic: they may not be much in themselves, but they are capable of adding a great deal to the value of everything else. —Dame Freya Madeleine Stark (1893–1993)

Coach Tressel says, "We encourage our players to exercise responsibility and right living by having class. Class is the way you carry yourself; it's not a socioeconomic designation. It's not about how much money you make or don't make. It's not a way to pigeonhole people.

Class is a way of life—a way of acting with confidence and style that reflects well on you and your team. It's having the freedom to do anything you want but choosing the right path."

It takes less time to do the right thing than to explain why you did it wrong. —Henry Wadsworth Longfellow

Conviction is worthless unless it is converted into conduct. —Thomas Carlyle

DO IT WITH CLASS

Class is respect for others. It is a deep and genuine respect for every human being, regardless of their status in life.

Class is having manners. It is always saying "thank you" and "please." It is complimenting people for any and every task well done.

Class is treating every other person as you would want them to treat you in a similar situation.

Class never makes excuses for one's own shortcomings, but it always helps others bounce back from their mistakes.

Class never brags or boasts about one's own accomplishments, and it never tears down or diminishes the achievements of another person.

Class does not depend on money, status, success, or ancestry. The wealthy aristocrat may not even know the meaning of the word, yet the poorest man in town may radiate *class* in everything he does.

If you have *class*, everyone will know it, and you will have self-respect. If you are without *class*—good luck because no matter what you accomplish, it will never have meaning.

Coach Tressel ends this fundamental by saying, "And when you think about it, that's what the fear of God is. I don't ever want to disappoint God. I want Him to be happy about the way I'm living my life, and I accomplish that with my commitment to finding out what 'doing right' is and then doing it."

#9—TEAM

(Together Everyone Achieves More)

Try to forget yourself in the service of others. For when we think too much of ourselves and our own interests, we easily become despondent. But when we work for others, our efforts return to bless us. —Sidney Powell

Unity is the great need of the hour, and if we are united, we can get many of the things that we not only desire but which we justly deserve. —Martin Luther King, Jr.

The nicest thing about teamwork is that you always have others on your side. —Margaret Carty

Coming together is a beginning; keeping together is a process; working together is a success. —Henry Ford

Coach Tressel reminds us, "If we really desire success, if we want the inner satisfaction and peace that comes from knowing we did all we could for the group, then we'll begin looking at the teams we're part of in a healthy way.

This is absolutely one of the most difficult things to do in today's society. We are fragmented and individualistic. Our personal computers and iPods and TV screens isolate us in our own little worlds."

Either we're pulling together, or we're pulling apart. There's really no in-between. —Kobi Yamada

OLD WARWICK

A man became lost while driving through the country. As he tried to read a map, he accidentally drove off the road into a ditch. Though he wasn't injured, his car was stuck deep in the mud. Seeing a farmhouse just down the road, the man walked over to ask for help.

"Warwick can get you out of the ditch," the farmer said, pointing to an old mule standing in a field. The man looked at the haggard mule and then looked back at the farmer, who just stood there nodding. "Yep, old Warwick can do the job."

The man figured he had nothing to lose, so the two men and Warwick made their way back to the ditch.

After the farmer hitched the old mule to the car, he snapped the reins and shouted, "Pull, Fred! Pull, Jack! Pull, Ted! Pull, Warwick!" With very little effort, the lone mule pulled the car from the ditch.

The man was amazed. He thanked the farmer, patted

the mule, and asked, “Why did you call out all those other names before you called Warwick?”

The farmer grinned and said, “Old Warwick is just about blind. As long as he believes he’s part of a team, he doesn’t mind pulling.”

Teamwork is a constant balancing act between self-interest and group interest. —Susan M. Campbell

#10—HOPE

Hope…is not the same as joy that things are going well or willingness to invest in enterprises that are obviously headed for early success, but rather, an ability to work for something because it is good, not just because it stands a chance to succeed. —Vaclav Havel, *Disturbing The Peace*

Live in your hopes and not in your fears. —Johnny Majors

There is no medicine like hope, no incentive so great, and no tonic so powerful as expectation of something tomorrow. —Orison Swett Marden (1850–1924)

Coach Tressel believes, “There are times in the game of life when it will seem as if things are not going very well. There are times when life departs from our familiar script and throws us something we had no idea was coming. It’s tempting in those circumstances to lose faith in ourselves, in the people around us, and even in God.

But if we’ve been planting the seeds of hope in our hearts, we’ll be able to overcome the problems of life and use them not only to make ourselves stronger but also to produce something good for ourselves and those we love.”

Hope is the feeling you have that the feeling you have isn’t permanent. —Jean Kerr

Coach T. goes on to say, “When we possess the hope and belief that ultimately, we’re going to be successful in our journeys, there's not much of what comes our way on a daily basis that we can't handle. When we see negative events as stepping stones and have hope that our problems can actually propel us toward our goals rather than hinder us, then we are, of all people, truly blessed. If I could pass along one virtue to all of our players—and to every reader of this version of the Winners Manual—it would be the virtue of *hope.*

Life is a series of ups and downs, peaks and valleys, wins and losses. When the bad times come, and they inevitably will, the seeds we've sown in our lives—what we believe in and hang on to and what we know is true and right—will help us maintain the hope that whatever stands before us is not permanent but only a temporary obstacle."

The human body experiences a powerful gravitational pull in the direction of hope. —Norman Cousins

Learning is discovering that something is possible. —Fritz Perls

Coach T. adds, "Knowledge is a wonderful thing. But *learning* means we take that raw knowledge and put it to work. When we learn and mature in knowledge, something takes place inside us that opens us up to a world of new possibilities.

As we go through phases of our lives, we all need the kind of hope that puts faith to work. It's sometimes easier to doubt ourselves and not move forward. Others will question the goals of the group, their roles in the group, or their direction in life."

Hope is putting faith to work when doubting would be easier. —Author Unknown

Coach T. goes on to say, "The type of hope I want to instill in my players is proactive and is based on reality, not on fantasy or wishful thinking.

It's not the kind of hope a person might have when buying

a lottery ticket with the last of the grocery money. Instead, it's a constant belief in the work that's already been done, the planning that's in place, and the potential that lies ahead.

The quotation by Andrew Fuller—*'Hope is one of the principal springs that keeps mankind in motion'*—tells me that if I choose, I can be a carrier of hope. Leaders do that. They take hope with them and pass it on to others. We have to make sure that in everything we do, we exemplify hope in our lives—especially on those days when things aren't going well. Others should be able to look at our lives and see the guiding light of hope within us that turns into outward action. It's important for others to see that there's a different way to live.

When people are devoid of hope, they're vulnerable to the traps of naysayers who think things can't be done and look at the world through negative lenses.

A person who hopes says, 'Sure, there are problems; yes, there are obstacles, but the future is bright—and with hard work, we can accomplish some great things.'

I have great hopes that the end result of reading this book will be a boost in the direction of the adventure, the confident search for a rewarding life. The power is not in my words or in the principles we've discovered; the power is in the opportunity you have to reflect on your life and evaluate your own purpose and goals. I've often said of our goal sheets that it's the thought process they provoke that makes the difference.

Moving forward and gaining confidence in our search for true success will be a lifelong endeavor. If we begin when we're young, we'll be able to see the changes we consciously make over the years, and we'll be better equipped to evaluate our progress.

But even if we're not so young anymore, we can begin

today to develop our purpose and set our goals for the years still to come."

Hope is an adventure, a going forward, a confident search for a rewarding life. —Karl Menninger

Focus on a hopeful future, not on self-pity. Self-pity is a trap that leads to deep depression. —Rosemarie Rossetti

If there were no hope, the heart would break. —Ancrene Wisse (CA. 1250)

Hope is one of those things in life you cannot do without. —Leroy Douglas

For I know the plans I have for you, says the LORD. They are plans for good and not for disaster, to give you a future and a hope. —Jeremiah 29:11 (NLT)

Coach Tressel ends this fundamental by saying, "If we can grasp the power of hope and then give that hope to those around us, we will see great things happen in our lives and in the lives of people we touch."

CHAPTER 3:
Becoming the Person Others Will Follow

Someone once said that if you think you're a leader and turn around to find no one is following you, then you are really just out for a long walk!

Known as America's expert on leadership, John Maxwell is the founder of the INJOY Group, an organization dedicated to helping people maximize their personal and leadership potential.

I had the privilege of meeting John years ago. I've attended quite a few of his leadership and stewardship seminars, and I've read just about every book he has written more than once! He has a wealth of knowledge on the subject of leadership, and it will be well worth your time to devour his wisdom on the topic of leadership.

In this chapter, we'll soak in a great deal of leadership wisdom from John Maxwell's book, *The 21 Indispensable Qualities of a Leader.*

1. CHARACTER:

First, the best definition of "character" I've ever heard comes from Andy Stanley: *"Character is the will to do what is right, as God defines right, regardless of personal cost."*

John Maxwell states, "The key to transforming yourself from someone who understands leadership to a person who successfully leads in the real world is character. Your character qualities activate and empower your leadership ability—or stand in the way of your success." A few points from Maxwell include:

- "Character is more than talk
- Talent is a gift, but character is a choice
- Character brings lasting success to people

- Leaders cannot rise above the limitations of their character
- As you lead others at home, at work, and in the community, recognize that your character is your most important asset."

2. CHARISMA:

"Charisma, plainly stated, is the ability to draw people to you. To make yourself the kind of person who attracts others, you need to personify these pointers:

- Love life
- Put a '10' on every person's head
- Give people hope
- Share yourself."

3. COMMITMENT:

"True commitment attracts and inspires people. It shows them that you have conviction. They will believe you only if you believe in your cause. People buy into the leader, then the vision."

4. COMMUNICATION:

"You can be more effective as a communicator if you follow four basic truths:

- Simplify your message
- See the person
- Show the truth
- Seek a response."

5. COMPETENCE:

If you want to cultivate the quality of competence, here's what you have to do:

- "Show up every day
- Keep improving
- Follow through with excellence
- Accomplish more than expected
- Inspire others."

6. COURAGE:

"As you approach the tough decisions that challenge you, recognize these truths about courage:

- Courage begins with an inward battle
- Courage is making things right, not just smoothing them over
- Courage in a leader inspires commitment from followers
- Your life expands in proportion to your courage."

7. DISCERNMENT:

"Discernment is an indispensable quality for any leader who desires to maximize effectiveness. It helps to do several important things:

- Discover the root issue
- Enhance your problem-solving
- Evaluate your opinions for maximum impact
- Multiply your opportunities."

8. FOCUS:

The keys to having "the focus required to be a truly effective leader are *priorities* and *concentration*. To improve your focus, do the following:

- Shift to strengths. Make a list of three or four things you do well in your job.
- Staff your weaknesses. Identify three or four activities necessary for your job that you don't do well.
- Create an edge. Time and money spent to take you to the next level are the best investment you can make."

9. GENEROSITY:

"Nothing speaks to others more loudly or serves them better than generosity from a leader. Cultivate the quality of generosity in your life. Here's how:

- Be grateful for whatever you have
- Put people first
- Don't allow the desire for possessions to control you
- Regard money as a resource
- Develop the habit of giving."

10. INITIATIVE:

Maxwell says there are at least four qualities "leaders possess that enable them to make things happen:

- They know what they want
- They push themselves to act
- They take more risks
- They make more mistakes."

11. LISTENING:

"A good leader encourages followers to tell him what he needs to know, not what he wants to hear…keep in mind that you have two purposes for listening: to connect with people and to learn. For that reason, you should keep your ear open to these people:

- Your followers
- Your customers
- Your competitors
- Your mentors."

12. PASSION:

Maxwell says there are "four truths about passion and what it can do for you as a leader:

- Passion is the first step to achievement
- Passion increases your willpower
- Passion changes you
- Passion makes the impossible possible."

13. POSITIVE ATTITUDE:

"A positive attitude not only determines your level of contentment as a person, but it also has an impact on how others interact with you.

- Your attitude is a choice.
- Your attitude determines your actions.
- Your people are a mirror of your attitude
- Maintaining a good attitude is easier than regaining one."

14. PROBLEM SOLVING:

"Leaders with good problem-solving abilities demonstrate five qualities:

- They anticipate problems
- They accept the truth
- They see the big picture
- They handle one thing at a time
- They don't give up on a major goal when they're down."

15. RELATIONSHIPS:

"It requires three things to manage and cultivate good relationships as a leader:

- Have a leader's head—Understand people
- Have a leader's heart—Love people
- Extend a leader's hand—Help people."

16. RESPONSIBILITY:

"Good leaders never embrace a victim mentality. They recognize that who and where they are remain their responsibility...characteristics of people who embrace responsibility:

- They get the job done
- They are willing to go the extra mile
- They are driven by excellence
- They produce regardless of the situation."

17. SECURITY:

- "Secure leaders are able to believe in others because they believe in themselves
- They aren't arrogant; they know their own strengths and weaknesses and respect themselves
- When their people perform well, they don't feel threatened
- They go out of their way to bring the best people together and then build them up so that they will perform at the highest level.
- When a secure leader's team succeeds, it brings him great joy. He sees that as the highest compliment he can receive for his leadership ability."

18. SELF-DISCIPLINE:

"If you want to become a leader for whom self-discipline is an asset, follow these action points:

- Develop and follow your priorities
- Make a disciplined lifestyle your goal
- Challenge your excuses
- Remove rewards until the job is done
- Stay focused on results."

19. SERVANTHOOD:

"A true servant leader:

- Puts others ahead of his own agenda
- Possesses the confidence to serve
- Initiates service to others
- Is not position-conscious
- Serves out of love."

20. TEACHABILITY:

"If you want to grow your organization, *you* have to remain teachable…five guidelines to help you cultivate and maintain a teachable attitude:

- Cure your destination disease
- Overcome your success
- Swear off shortcuts
- Trade in your pride
- Never pay twice for the same mistake."

21. VISION:

"A great leader's courage to fulfill his vision comes from passion, not position. To get a handle on vision and how it comes to be part of a good leader's life, understand these things:

- Vision starts within
- Vision draws on your history
- Vision meets other's needs
- Vision helps you gather resources."

CHAPTER 4:
Follow These Laws and People Will Follow You

In this chapter, we're going to glean more wisdom on leadership from John Maxwell's book, *The 21 Irrefutable Laws of Leadership*. Maxwell says, "*Everything rises and falls on leadership.* These laws carry consequences with them. Apply the laws, and people will follow you. Violate or ignore them, and you will not be able to lead others. The good news is every one of the 21 laws of leadership can be learned."

1. THE LAW OF THE LID: Maxwell believes The Law of the Lid is the most important leadership principle we will ever learn. Maxwell states, "Leadership ability is always the lid on personal and organizational effectiveness. If the leadership is strong, the lid is high. But if it's not, then the organization is limited. That's why in times of trouble, organizations naturally look for new leadership."
2. THE LAW OF INFLUENCE: "The true measure of leadership is influence—nothing more, nothing less. True leadership cannot be awarded, appointed, or assigned. It comes only from influence, and that can't be mandated. It must be earned."
3. THE LAW OF PROCESS: "Successful leaders are learners. Leadership develops daily, not in a day."
4. THE LAW OF NAVIGATION: "First-rate navigators always have in mind that other people are depending on them and their ability to chart a good course."
5. THE LAW OF E. F. HUTTON: "When the real leader speaks, people listen."
6. THE LAW OF SOLID GROUND: "Trust is the foundation of leadership. People will tolerate honest

mistakes, but if you violate their trust, you will find it very difficult to ever regain their confidence."

7. THE LAW OF RESPECT: "People naturally follow leaders stronger than themselves."
8. THE LAW OF INTUITION: "Leaders see everything with a leadership bias, and as a result, they instinctively, almost automatically, know what to do. The great ones can see things others can't, make changes, and move forward before others know what's happening."
9. THE LAW OF MAGNETISM: "Who you are is who you attract. In most situations, you draw people to you who possess the same qualities as you do."
10. THE LAW OF CONNECTION: "Leaders touch a heart before they ask for a hand. The greatest leaders are able to connect on both levels: with individuals and with an audience."
11. THE LAW OF THE INNER CIRCLE: "A leader's potential is determined by those closest to him. If those people are strong, then the leader can make a huge impact. If they are weak, he can't."
12. THE LAW OF EMPOWERMENT: "Only secure leaders give power to others. The number one enemy of empowerment is the desire for job security."
13. THE LAW OF REPRODUCTION: "It takes a leader to raise up a leader. People cannot give to others what they themselves do not possess. Followers simply cannot develop leaders."
14. THE LAW OF BUY-IN: "Every message that people receive is filtered through the messenger who delivers it. If you consider the messenger to be credible, then you believe the message has value."

15. THE LAW OF VICTORY: "Victory is possible as long as you have three components:

    a. Unity of vision

    b. Diversity of skills

    c. A leader dedicated to victory and raising players to their potential."

16. THE LAW OF BIG MO: "Strong leaders understand that to change direction, you first have to create forward progress. When leadership is strong and there is momentum in an organization, people are motivated and inspired to perform at higher levels."

17. THE LAW OF PRIORITIES: "Leaders understand that activity is not necessarily accomplishment. To be effective, leaders must order their lives according to these three questions:

    a. What is required?

    b. What gives the greatest return?

    c. What brings the greatest reward?"

18. THE LAW OF SACRIFICE: "Usually, the higher that the leader has climbed, the greater the sacrifice he has made. Effective leaders sacrifice much that is good in order to dedicate themselves to what is best." Just a caveat on these quotes: knowing John Maxwell as I do, he would not advocate sacrificing your health, your marriage, or your family relationships for the sake of climbing the corporate ladder!

19. THE LAW OF TIMING: "When to lead is just as important as what to do and where to go. Only the right action *at the right time* will bring success. Anything else exacts a high price."

20. THE LAW OF EXPLOSIVE GROWTH: "To add growth, lead followers—to multiply, lead leaders."

21. THE LAW OF LEGACY: “A leader’s lasting value is measured by succession. A legacy is created only when a person puts his organization in the position to do great things *without* him.”

CHAPTER 5: Leadership vs. Management

The Difference That Will Change the Way You Work

Posted on February 2, 2020, by Lindsay Pietroluongo

Managers can be leaders, and leaders can be managers, but when you get down to it, there are significant differences between the roles. Leaders may or may not have authority, but they always find a way to push people forward—to lead them to where they should go. On the other hand, managers direct employees on what to do and how to do it. They keep the business running like a well-oiled machine. Let's talk about leadership vs management and how you can combine the best of both worlds for the sake of your business.

What is a Leader?

Leaders showcase and share their vision to inspire the people around them. They're driven by passion. They don't mind a bit of chaos and a lack of structure. Leaders tend to:

- Change the expectations and moods of customers
- Delay solving a problem so they can better understand its causes
- Pay attention to ethical behavior
- Set goals based on desires
- Understand and visualize the purpose and value of work
- Use empathy and intuition to relate to people

What is a Manager?

Managers protect the structure of an organization. They control how the workplace runs, and they strike the correct balance of power.

They believe in persistence and hard work—in rolling up their sleeves and getting it done. Managers tend to:

- Build competence in employees
- Have an analytical mind
- Look for control and stability
- Resolve problems fast (even if they don't understand the significance of a problem)
- Set goals based on the company's culture and history
- Take a tactical approach to get work done in a timely manner

Leadership vs Management: The Main Differences You Should Know About

Leadership is what pushes a company forward to reach goals and succeed, and management is what keeps a company running like a machine. You need both roles filled, and knowing the distinct differences between them will help you get the balance right.

Motivations

The biggest difference between leadership and management is motivation, which is best illustrated in how each type of person sets goals. Leaders set goals based on shaping ideas instead of reacting to demand. Managers set more straightforward and practical goals based on history and forecasting.

A leader may set a goal to create or enhance a product that will meet the needs of customers, even if customers don't realize they have those needs yet. This type of goal is less predictable and reliable than a manager's goal, but the risk means there's potential for huge growth.

A manager may set a goal to have a certain amount of product available in a specific store by a set date in order to meet customer demand. This type of goal may not perform as well as a riskier goal that takes off, but the tried-and-true approach can mean guaranteed cash flow.

Risk

Leaders purposely seek out risk and danger, while managers work hard to minimize risk. Leaders prefer growing pains to stagnancy or tradition, especially if a potential reward is on the other side. Managers don't see anything more than the danger that comes with risk—they don't notice the opportunities like leaders do. That's not to say that managers are worse than leaders; companies need to balance risk and reliability to grow in a sustainable way.

Work Tasks

Leaders are often more creative than straightforward managers. Leadership takes an imaginative approach rather than a clinical one. Managers have an easier time handling mundane work, like administrative tasks and analytical tasks, than leaders; leaders can almost seem allergic to that type of work.

Influence

There are different types of influence when it comes to leadership vs management. A leader can influence what a customer wants by coming up with novel ideas and solutions. They wait to see how audiences respond, and if they respond well, they dig deeper to round out the options and deliver what's best for the customer.

The type of influence a manager has is more manipulative (though not in a bad way). They can influence the decisions people make by framing the choices to point to the correct ones. Managers are able to subconsciously steer people—employees or customers—to make the choice the manager wants them to make.

For example, when you want to buy software, you'll choose from tiered packages. The middle package is usually highlighted in some way. The customer loves it because it offers the best value for their money. It's also the best option for the company. The cost is higher than the cheapest package, and subscribers are more likely to stick with it than the pricier option. The customer thinks they're making the choice, but their company leads them straight to it.

How to Combine Leadership and Management in a Company

It's not necessarily leaders who climb the ranks to become managers—the succession of power doesn't always coincide with who's a good leader. In that way, you can have leaders who don't move up in their careers and high-level managers who aren't skilled at leading. That's okay, so long as you have both roles filled at a company and leaders are given a lot of freedom to make a difference. Here's how to build a company that has equal parts leadership and management.

Offer the Proper Training for Leadership vs Management

Since management relies so much on structure, process, and doing things a certain way, it's a lot easier to train someone to be a manager than to be a leader. Leadership is more innate than management. It's possible to teach and enhance some aspects of leadership, but, for the most part, people are inherently leaders (or not), and they may not even know how skilled they are at leadership until they see how they naturally influence others. That said, leadership skills *can* develop over time through experience and practice and even through purposeful self-development, like taking leadership training courses.

Clarify Each Employee's Purpose

After (or before) telling employees what's expected of them and teaching them how to do it, explain why they're carrying out certain functions. What is the purpose of their role? What are they adding to the company?

Show that Progress is Always the Goal

You can illustrate that continued progress is the company's main goal when the business is doing well and even when something's gone wrong. For example, once goals are reached for the quarter, come up with new goals to work on until it's time to start on the next quarter's regular goals. Or, maybe something has failed. Managers are excellent at taking the next realistic step forward but also ask themselves and the team what that failure's learning lessons are.

Create an Accepting Work Environment

In an open work atmosphere, employees feel like it's okay to approach higher-ups with different ideas. They may have discovered a way to do their job better, or they could have a suggestion for improving a process. Or, they may question why certain rules are in place, in which case management should consider whether a rule should be hard-and-fast or a more flexible guideline.

Set Up a System for Applying New Ideas

Simply gathering ideas isn't enough. There should be a process for adding new ideas to the mix, one or two at a time, that go through a trial basis before becoming a permanent part of processes. Risks should be taken, even if they're taken in measured amounts, while the rest of the company runs as usual.

Rethink Leadership vs Management Communication Styles

A manager tells an employee they did a great job by saying, "Great job." A leader adds more personalization and emotion. For example, "Fantastic job! I can always count on you to come through." Before sending off an email, take an extra minute to quickly revise it and warm it up.

How Leaders Can Influence Management Without Overstepping Boundaries

Typically, leaders don't care about control and organization, but managers do. Managers can feel threatened by leaders—even leaders who can positively impact the business—because disorder is bound to follow. Managers may also feel that their level of authority is being challenged when, really, it's just their approach or idea that's being challenged.

While leaders focus on risk and change, that has to be properly communicated to management so approval can be given to move forward. The potential outcome can be framed in a way that the manager can understand and analyze.

For example, a leader may say, "If we try XYZ, there's a possibility we'll see this percentage of growth. Here's an example of a competitor that did something similar and how they benefited."

Final Thoughts on Leadership vs Management

While logic and strategy are necessary, creativity and inventiveness may be considered more important, and they should be allowed to be stoked and grow. At the same time, a company that is solely run by creativity and imagination won't have the structure needed for analysis and operations. When you're able to have leaders and managers working together, you'll increase productivity, improve communication, develop better relationships, and boost the workplace overall.

CHAPTER 6: (25) Things Influential People Do Well

Influential people are all around us, and they usually have one area of expertise in which they excel. Despite their differences in topic and subject matter, influencers across the board tend to have similar characteristics. They do certain things better than others—not necessarily because they want to, but because they have to. If they didn't, their influence would cease to exist.

Every influencer has these 25 attributes to varying degrees. And if they don't, you can bet they're working on them.

1. *Public speaking.* In order to grow and maintain influence, many influencers turn to public speaking. It's a great way to get their face out there and stick in their audience's mind.
2. *Prioritizing.* Influencers are able to prioritize the parts of their life that bring them the most joy and success and minimize the parts that don't.
3. *Small talk.* This is like public speaking, but a very different skill set. Small talk means taking an interest in the small things in life and making the person they're talking to really feel listened to.
4. *Remembering details.* Influencers have a way of remembering tiny (but very important) details about the things they're passionate about.
5. *Smiling.* Let your friendliness shine through, whether you are online or offline.
6. *Persuading.* Influencers are able to persuade their audiences of nearly anything (within reason). And it's usually due to one thing: trust. Their audience trusts their recommendations, and so they allow themselves to be persuaded. An influencer without trust is no influencer at all.

7. *Confidence.* Influential people have faith in themselves. Sure, they take huge risks, but only because they have the confidence that they'll land on their feet.
8. *Conversions.* Influencers are able to convert audience members into clients and fast.
9. *Setting expectations.* When people know what to expect, they're less likely to be disappointed, and influencers know this. Influential people establish clear parameters of who they are, what they do, and how they act, and they don't make any sudden changes to this formula.
10. *Energizing.* There's just something about influencers that makes your heart beat a little faster, and your mind snaps into high gear. They're great at energizing—themselves, a room full of people listening to their keynote, a client, anyone!
11. *Body language.* Influencers act like their actions are effortless, and that's a lot of work! If you think they're always well put-together and their posture is picture-perfect even at home, think again. They make a point to express themselves fully, in their words as well as their body language, and that's a big part of their charisma.
12. *Networking.* Knowing who's who is one thing, but being the who's who is even better! Influencers are usually a central figure within a large, engaged network, and they got there because they worked at it. They built connections, fostered relationships, and paid it forward.
13. *Multitasking.* Sending an email, chatting to a client on the phone, and dealing with a crowded airport, all at the same time, is just another day in the life of influencers. They're great at doing a dozen things at once without ever letting a single ball drop.

14. *Flexibility.* Influencers have to be able to change if they want to remain relevant. Whether it's adopting a new tool or altering their personal brand, the most influential people are flexible enough to know when to take a new stance.

15. *Timing.* Knowing when to make a move is just as important as actually making it. Influencers have great timing in nearly all of their decisions. Do they switch from Apple to Android? The actual switch might not matter as much as the timing, depending on the influencer!

16. *Giving compliments.* Influencers are generous people at heart. They dole out compliments all the time—and they're usually genuine, too!

17. *Technology.* Influencers always seem to have the latest gadgets, apps, and tech at their fingertips. They stay on top of technology trends (or at least have people who do that for them), and they use the latest tech to optimize their time.

18. *Preparing for clients/events.* Preparation is half the battle. Influencers don't jump into anything blind if they can be prepared for it. Before any event, big or small, influencers will make sure they're as prepared as possible. This might mean reading up on old emails, doing research online, preparing notes, and taking calls. They'll do what it takes to understand the situation and conquer it.

19. *Travel.* Influencers are always on the go, so they have to become travel pros by default. They use their tech and their time wisely while on the road, so not a single second is wasted… even in an excruciatingly long security line.

20. *Reciprocating.* Business is about relationships, and influencers know this. A great influencer will adopt a

philosophy of reciprocity—they give as good as they get! In all of their business relationships, they strive to offer value in order to capture value in return, creating win-win situations for everyone involved.

21. *Kindness.* They know jerks don't do well in the long run. Just being nice can go a long way in winning fans and influence.

22. *Balancing.* Even if they don't have a work/life balance, you'd never know it because they give every impression of being perfectly Zen. Influencers have a lot on the go, and the best are able to manage it all without breaking a sweat. Work, kids, hobbies, travel… they balance their otherwise hectic lives with ease (or at least they make it look easy!).

23. *Always being "on."* Influencers know they have to put their best face forward all the time to maintain their status.

24. *Constructive criticism.* If you can dish it, they can take it. Influencers are able to take criticism in stride and use it to make themselves better. They don't respond to trolls, but if someone has a genuine criticism of how they conduct their business, they'll listen.

25. *BackStory.* Whatever yours is, theirs is better. They've built their empire from the ground up, and that's part of their appeal. Influencers are great at pulling the best parts of their past together for a compelling backstory that could probably be made into a feature film.

CHAPTER 7:
(25) Business Skills to Master Now!

In today's competitive work environment, if you want to stand out as a job applicant or an employee competing for a promotion, there are certain skills you must bring to the table to impress employers.

The following information written by a staff writer for the *Get Motivated Workbook* will help you take an inventory of your current skill set. You'll be able to access your current strengths as well as the areas where you may need some work.

In the article, Randall S. Hansen states, "Whether you're seeking your first job, a new opportunity, or a promotion within your current company, the business skills you need to master are the same.

Beyond evaluating job-specific requirements, employers look for 'hard skills' and 'soft skills' in a candidate seeking a position or promotion."

Stay ahead of the curve in your career by brushing up on each of these 25 vital skills.

Hard Skills

1. COMMUNICATION: Vitally important in business, successful communication includes concise writing, careful listening, and effective speaking—all of which will be evaluated in your resume and interviews.
2. ANALYTICAL: This skill begins with the ability to see the big picture, assess a situation, gather information, seek multiple perspectives, and then apply sound judgment.
3. COMPUTER/TECHNICAL: If you don't possess solid computer skills, get them or be left behind.

4. ADAPTIVE: As employers downsize and combine jobs, they are focusing on efficiency. Show your value by demonstrating a willingness to learn new skills and assume additional responsibilities.
5. INTERPERSONAL: The workplace is all about people. If you're an alpha male or female, tone it down. Learn to understand and accept different personalities.
6. LEADERSHIP/MANAGEMENT: Whether you've progressed to a management position yet or not, your leadership skills are important because they demonstrate initiative. "Don't wait to be told to do a job or take on a responsibility," advises Shelly Field, author of *The Unofficial Guide to Hot Careers*. She says, "A willingness to take the lead or solve a problem will get you noticed."
7. MULTICULTURAL SENSITIVITY: As the workplace grows more diverse every day, show you can get along with people from different backgrounds. Multicultural sensitivity has become an employability hot button.
8. PLANNING/ORGANIZATION: Demonstrate your ability to take a task from beginning to end and finish it on time.
9. PROBLEM SOLVING: Creative problem-solving is important at all levels of any organization. Document your best examples for your next interview.
10. TEAMWORK: "Valuable employees are team players committed to the organization's goals," says Laura Berman Fortgang, author of *Living Your Best Life*.

Soft Skills

1. LOYALTY: Managers facing staff cuts, with no reduction in workload, are keenly aware of who's with them and who's not.
2. INTEGRITY: As corporate scandals rock news headlines, it's not surprising that integrity tops the list of personal values employers are seeking in employees.
3. FLEXIBILITY: Become a star player by demonstrating a willingness to leave your comfort zone.
4. DEDICATION: By showing care for your work and concern for your company, you will be valued for your commitment and for the example you set.
5. RELIABILITY: Prove you can be counted on, so you won't be easily counted out when the chips are down.
6. POSITIVE ATTITUDE: Particularly when times are tough, your positive attitude will boost morale for everyone and make you an essential member of the team.
7. PROFESSIONALISM: A code of conduct and a sign of maturity, professionalism covers a host of behaviors, from being fair and responsible to never being petty.
8. SELF-CONFIDENCE: If you don't believe in yourself, who will?
9. WILLINGNESS TO LEARN: Jobs are constantly evolving, so demonstrate that you can, too, no matter your age or level of experience.
10. ABILITY TO WORK INDEPENDENTLY: A counterpart to teamwork, being a self-starter who performs well with minimal demands on a supervisor's time will distinguish you in today's competitive job arena.

11. RESPECT FOR OTHERS: Every person you interact with during your workday, from the CEO to the receptionist, gives you an opportunity to demonstrate respect, which others will reflect back on you.
12. PATIENCE: Wrapped up in our own immediate needs, it's easy to forget those of others. Show respect by being patient.
13. A GOOD LISTENER: Listening is a sign of respect and patience for others.
14. WILLINGNESS TO CONDUCT RESEARCH: Go the extra mile to learn all you can, and then question what you learn. Just because something comes up on Google doesn't make it true!
15. TIME MANAGEMENT: The more effectively you manage your time, the better you will become at meeting your goals and those of your company.

CHAPTER 8: Problem-Solving Made Easy

Next, we're going to gain some very useful wisdom from Tim Hansel's book, *Eating Problems for Breakfast*.

Hansel says, "Too often our schools have focused their teachings on *what* to think rather than on *how* to think… Few people have a strategy for solving problems…When problems arise at inconvenient times, most of us react rather than respond." Hansel believes "our ability to solve problems depends on our attitude, our approach, our skill, and our experience. As Chuck Swindoll said so eloquently, 'We are all faced with a series of great opportunities brilliantly disguised as impossible situations.'"

The Purpose of Problems

Hansel goes on to say, "Ingrained in our thinking are three false ideas about problems. It is these that I believe cause us to miss the creative purpose of problems.

- *False Idea Number 1:* We believe that there is something inherently bad about problems because they often involve us in unpleasant pressures, distressing conflicts, or an inconvenient interruption of our plans for a smooth and easy life.
- *False Idea Number 2:* We think that lack of problems should be a reward for hard work, careful planning, and clear thinking. Present in each of us is the hope that eventually—out ahead somewhere, sometime—our life will be free of problems of any kind.
- *False Idea Number 3:* We think that if we love God, commit our lives to Him, and diligently serve Him, He will work things out for us so that everything will run smoothly for us and we will be free from problems.

When it doesn't work that way, we ask why is this or that happening to us.

Problems are the very means by which God changes us, transforms us, and drives us forward. Without problems, there would be no growth."

The Qualities of a Good Problem Solver

The qualities of good problem solvers include:

- Having *"confidence in their ability to learn and their ability to solve problems."*
- A tendency *"to enjoy solving problems."*
- Relying "*on their own judgment.* Though they know there is wisdom in much counsel, they respect their own decision-making abilities."
- Not being "*fast answerers*. Although they don't procrastinate on decisions, they don't make hasty decisions either. Before making any decision, they gather as much data as they can."
- Being *"flexible and are often capable of seeing more than one answer to a question or problem."*
- Knowing *"the difference between fact and opinion and having a high degree of respect for fact."*
- Not needing *"to have an absolute, final, irrevocable solution to every problem.* They know that the only thing that is constant is change."
  The Ten Commandments of Problem Solving

1. *Challenge Assumptions:* "To assume is to think that you already know. What some people call 'thinking' is simply a rearranging of their prejudices…Assumptions result from limited information or from looking at a problem from the wrong angle.

Oftentimes, assumptions are faulty interpretations of the given facts, frequently occurring when we look only on the surface of things."

2. *Keep a Large Perspective:* "Learn to look at problems from different angles. Ask tough questions. See all that is there—see the problem as it *really* is in all its fullness."
3. *Don't Get Hooked:* "Emotions are good. But emotions also have the power to disrupt our lives seriously when we allow them to control us. You are probably emotionally hooked when your emotions are in control when you can no longer think logically. Another good sign that you're hooked is when you use words like 'always' and 'never'; you state your point in exaggerations and generalizations; you magnify the problem way out of proportion; you want emotional satisfaction more than a solution to the problem."
4. *Simple Is Better:* "Simple answers are not necessarily simplistic answers...simplistic answers don't address the real issues of a problem. If you use them, you will probably cover up what you don't understand rather than take the time to see the problem clearly. To simplify a problem means simply to remove that which clutters up your thinking."
5. *Look for the Second Right Answer:* "People try to avoid problems by acting on their first impulse rather than by trying to discover alternate solutions. There are several dangers to this impulsive method of problem-solving. First, acting on the first right answer limits us to one course of action, while discovering other possible solutions creates multiple possibilities and increases flexibility. Second, an idea or a solution is best understood in the context of other ideas. If we have only one idea, we can't

compare it to anything else, so we don't know its strengths and weaknesses."

6. *Ask Dumb Questions:* "Problem-solving is basically a process of asking questions. The tougher the problem, the better the questions must be. In reality, there is no such thing as a dumb question. In fact, sometimes the simplest and most obvious questions (those that seem dumb) are often the most profound."

7. *Unlock Your Creativity:* "Being creative means taking everyday material and turning it into something extraordinary.

Creativity isn't just for the selected few. Since there is nothing new under the sun, it means simply putting old things together in a new and fresh way. Creativity is especially expressed in the ability to make connections, to make associations, to turn things around and express them in a new way."

8. *Scratch Where It Itches:* "Before you can solve a problem, it is critical that you understand what the problem really is. Don't waste time scratching where it doesn't itch. What is the priority in this problem? What are the core issues? What is the central focus? We need to concentrate on the essentials, eliminating everything that is unnecessary. Look at the problem rather than the symptoms."

9. *Make It Fun:* "Having fun releases our problem-solving abilities and gives us a much more objective and flexible frame of reference. It allows us to play with ideas, use principles (such as reversal), and expect the unexpected. Making life fun and making problem-solving fun allows you to embrace change, even to love change, to enjoy it, and to get excited about the challenges that face you."

10. *Hang in There:* "It's been said a thousand different ways. Never give up. Stick to it. Be stubborn. Persevere. Don't quit. Go the second mile. Hang in there. Invest time in your problem. In fact, ninety percent of all failures result from people quitting too soon.

Hansen believes there is a repeatable seven-step process to solving any problem. He says, "This seven-step process is appropriate to any problem, whether it be fixing a kitchen door or a relationship at work, whether it be solving a logistical hassle or working with some disruption in your family. It works on all kinds of problems—and it is so logical that if you were to write these seven steps down and practice them, even for a few days, they would become automatic to you."

Seven-Step Problem-Solving Process

1. *"Recognize and accept a problem.* You must first realize a problem exists and be willing to engage yourself fully in an attempt to correct it. This, believe it or not, is one of the most important steps in problem-solving. It is the beginning point of all problem-solving.
2. *Analyze the problem.* Take it apart, simplify it, and get to know the ins and outs of the problem. See each of its pieces with as much clarity as possible.
3. *Define the problem.* What really is the problem? Eliminate anything that is unnecessary. What do you believe are the main issues of the problem? Clarify the major goals to solve the problem. It helps if you can write out the problem or state it clearly to another person.
4. *Brainstorm.* Generate as many ideas or potential answers as you can. If possible, brainstorm with another person. Write down every idea you think of. Quantity is more important than quality at this point.

5. *Select.* Choose what appears to be the best possible way of solving the problem at this time. Try to select between the best alternatives, taking the most logical solution at this time.
6. *Implement.* Try it out. Put into action your selected best choice.
7. *Evaluate.* Determine the effect or results of the solution in correcting the problem. Did it work? If not, what could you do to improve the solution at this time?

This means problem-solving is a continuing process or journey. If you finish the seven steps and are still unsatisfied, then you automatically go back to the beginning, to the first step, with a new sense of awareness. Remember that each of these steps or phases are *interrelated*, forming a continuous journey—the more we practice them, the more natural they become. If we wish to improve our problem-solving abilities, we must work toward improving and developing each step or phase in the problem-solving process.

Use this problem-solving process in your everyday life. You might be surprised to discover a new sense of clarity and direction unfolding in your life. Remember, the test of character isn't always how we handle the big problems but how we deal with the ordinary ones as well."

CHAPTER 9:
Entrepreneurial Wisdom for Starting a Business

If you've ever thought about starting your own business, one of the first things you *MUST* do prior to just jumping in and hoping for the best is to start watching *Shark Tank*, if you don't already!

Amber Dawn MacArthur, who goes by Amber Mac, is a Canadian television and net casting personality. She is also a tech entrepreneur, keynote speaker, bestselling author, and TV host.

Below is an article she wrote about *Shark Tank* that includes a great deal of wisdom for anyone with an entrepreneurial spirit.

7 Entrepreneurial Lessons From "Shark Tank"

Shark Tank, the prime-time feeding frenzy where successful entrepreneurs fight over promising startups and ruthlessly chew up the unprepared, provides a wealth of knowledge about what venture capitalists need to hear before they invest in your company.

With billionaire Mark Cuban, real estate mogul Barbara Corcoran, venture capitalist Kevin O'Leary (AKA Mr. Wonderful), and other business magnates sitting in as the Sharks, the show offers a glimpse of pitching sessions gone totally right—or deliciously wrong.

An example: When three ice cream makers first lined up in front of the Sharks to pitch their product, they generated some friendly conversation. After all, the concept of morphing together beer and America's favorite frozen treat is bound to appeal to our inner glutton. However, when the investors started asking the entrepreneurs tough questions about their finances, the men from The Brewer's Cow had a minor meltdown. Whether the Connecticut-based founders were the victims of calculated editing or simply unprepared, their presentation lacked a certain professionalism. The final verdict? A flurry of "I'm outs" from the Sharks.

Yes, the episodes are entertaining. But more than that, they provide a wealth of knowledge about what venture capitalists want to hear before they invest in your company—and what will turn them off. Here are seven lessons from the Sharks about learning what it takes to make it as an entrepreneur.

1. *Know your numbers.* This is the number one lesson from *Shark Tank*. Whether you're presenting to a team of investors or simply working to grow your business, it's critical that you understand how much cash is coming in and out of the business. While you might think that most entrepreneurs on Shark Tank have a handle on their books, many believe that their passion will sell their wares. However, as we've learned from many of the Sharks, passion only gets you so far—numbers tell the real story.
2. *Be a good marketer.* Although the boys from The Brewer's Cow didn't get the deal they wanted, there is no doubt that the exposure from the show is extremely valuable. However, as a Shark Tank fan shares on his blog, the company's website is pretty lackluster for a brand that hopes to go national. If you extend the online search to their Twitter feed, there has been very little interaction since the show aired. The Brewer's Cow currently has a deal with Whole Foods, but on the online front, there is a lot more they could be doing just days after the television broadcast to capitalize from the on-air buzz.
3. *Be humble.* When a young entrepreneur appeared on the show to sell his custom clothing, he expressed the

business drive that the Sharks love, but things started to fall apart when he talked about his lifestyle. Aside from asking for a starting six-figure salary (when the company has only grossed just over $315,000), he also lost some Sharks when he declared, "I'm now living the L.A. life." As Shark Damond John, founder of FUBU, expressed on his Twitter feed, a statement like this isn't very appealing to a potential investor looking to form a responsible partnership.

4. *Understand good timing.* There are good and bad times in your business to ask for investment money. Many of the companies diving into the Shark Tank have great ideas, but it's too early on in their businesses to be on the hunt for a large amount of cash.
5. Mom Raven Thomas was one of the most impressive entrepreneurs on the show in terms of leaking out little bits of information about her business to entice the Sharks, one by one. For example, when she shared that Sam's Club recently put in an order for $2 million for her chocolate-covered pretzels, she had Cuban drooling to seal a deal.
6. *Have a good story.* When Travis Perry explained his company's motivation to the Sharks, it tugged on their inner musician heartstrings. Perry invented his product Chordbuddy to help new guitar players like his 10-year-old daughter avoid frustration when learning how to play the popular instrument. With a great story and a stellar product, Perry got investment help and now has his Chordbuddy product in more than 100 music stores.
7. *Be prepared to walk.* Some things are not meant to be, which was the case with entrepreneur Scott Jordan. As founder of the successful brands SCOTTEVEST and TEC, he appeared on the show to sell a percentage

of the latter (a technology-enabled clothing patent). The Sharks, on the other hand, were interested in Jordan's main business, SCOTTEVEST, which is on track to make more than $20 million this year. After a heated debate with some of the Sharks, Jordan was happy to walk away without a deal but with some new publicity for both his businesses.

8. *Be personable.* While all of the above will get you closer to your dream of running a successful business, it also helps to have a winning personality. No one wants to do business with someone who is unlikable, except maybe Mr. Wonderful. As Shark Barbara Corcoran said in a recent tweet, "All the entrepreneurs I've invested in have amazing personalities—no regrets."

Remember all those things you learned about being nice in kindergarten? Those same things apply in the boardroom, with no exceptions!

CHAPTER 10: Secrets to Success for Any Path You Choose in Life

I'm concerned today's obsession with computers, cell phones, texting, Twitter, Facebook, Instagram, Snapchat, and other communication apps are seriously hindering real face-to-face communication, especially among students of all ages and young adults.

Just go to any coffee shop or restaurant where students and young adults hang out and see for yourself. More often than not, rather than interacting verbally with one another, they have their eyes glued to their cell phones, either chatting or texting with someone else, surfing on Facebook, or playing games!

John D. Rockefeller was one of the richest men in the world. When talking about what it takes to be successful in business and in life, Rockefeller said, "The ability to deal with people is as purchasable a commodity as sugar or coffee. And I will pay more for that ability than for any other under the sun."

Famed author and lecturer Dale Carnegie said, "The person who has technical knowledge *plus* the ability to express ideas, to assume leadership, and to arouse enthusiasm among people—that person is headed for higher earning power."

I'm concerned many high school students, college students, and young adults already attempting to climb their corporate ladders are terribly ill-prepared to achieve their desired goals at work and in life due to a lack of proper communication skills, both verbal and written.

In this chapter, I'd like to give you some insight into the wisdom millions of people around the world have found to help them become extremely successful in the business world and life in general.

Dale Carnegie's book, *How to Win Friends and Influence People*, was first published in 1937 with only 5,000 copies. The book literally became an international best-seller overnight.

On the cover of his book I own, it says, "Almost 15,000,000 copies have been sold in all editions, and those editions include translations into virtually every language." With all these books in circulation around the world, I'm still amazed at how many folks I know have never read this tremendously educational book!

There are at least eight things this book will help you achieve:

1. Get out of a mental rut, think new thoughts, acquire new visions, and discover new ambitions.
2. Make friends quickly and easily.
3. Increase your popularity.
4. Win people to your way of thinking.
5. Increase your influence, your prestige, and your ability to get things done.
6. Handle complaints, avoid arguments, and keep your human contacts smooth and pleasant.
7. Become a better speaker and a more entertaining conversationalist.
8. Arouse enthusiasm among your associates.

Fundamental Techniques in Handling People

Principle 1: "Don't Criticize, Condemn or Complain—Criticism is dangerous because it wounds a person's precious pride, hurts his sense of importance, and arouses resentment. The resentment that criticism engenders can demoralize employees, family members, and friends and still not correct the situation that has been condemned.

Instead of condemning people, let's try to understand them. Let's try to figure out why they do what they do. That's a lot more profitable and intriguing than criticism, and it breeds sympathy, tolerance, and kindness."

Principle 2: "Give Honest, Sincere Appreciation— Charles Schwab was only thirty-eight years old when he was hired and paid over a million dollars a year to become the first president of the newly formed United States Steel Company in 1921. Schwab says he was paid this salary largely because of his ability to deal with people. 'I consider my ability to arouse enthusiasm among my people,' said Schwab, 'the greatest asset I possess, and the way to develop the best that is in a person is by appreciation and encouragement.' There is nothing else that so kills the ambition of a person as criticism from superiors." An excellent lesson for parents to learn as well.

*Principle 3: "Arouse in the Other Person an Eager Want—*There is only one way under high heaven to get anybody to do anything. And that is by making the other person want to do it." Henry Ford said, "If there is any one secret of success, it lies in the ability to get the other person's point of view and see things from that person's angle as well as from your own." Carnegie goes on to say, "The world is full of people who are grabbing and self-seeking. So, the rare individual who unselfishly tries to serve others has an enormous advantage. He has little competition."

Six Ways to Make People Like You

*PRINCIPLE 1: "Become Genuinely Interested in Other People—*Do this, and you'll be welcome anywhere. You can make more friends in two months by becoming interested in other people than you can in two years by trying to get other people interested in you. If you want others to like you, if you want to develop real friendships, if you want to help others at the same time as you help yourself, become genuinely interested in them."

PRINCIPLE 2: "Smile—A simple way to make a good first impression. The expression one wears on one's face is far more important than the clothes one wears on one's back. You must have a good time meeting people if you expect them to have a good time meeting you. Everybody in the world is seeking happiness, and there is one sure way to find it. That is by controlling your thoughts. Happiness doesn't depend on outward conditions. It depends on inner conditions. Your smile is a messenger of your goodwill."

PRINCIPLE 3: "Remember That a Person's Name is to That Person the Sweetest and Most Important Sound in Any Language—The executive who tells me he can't remember names is at the same time telling me he can't remember a significant part of his business and is operating on quicksand. The average person is more interested in his or her own name than in all the other names on earth put together. Remember that name and call it easily, and you have paid a subtle and very effective compliment. But forget it or misspell it, and you have placed yourself at a sharp disadvantage."

PRINCIPLE 4: "Be a Good Listener—Encourage others to talk about themselves. Many people fail to make a favorable impression because they don't listen attentively. They have been so much concerned with what they are going to say next that they do not keep their ears open. Very important people have told me that they prefer good listeners to good talkers, but the ability to listen seems rarer than almost any other good trait. To be interesting, be interested. Ask questions that other people will enjoy answering. Encourage them to talk about themselves and their accomplishments."

PRINCIPLE 5: "Talk in Terms of the Other Person's Interests—When Theodore Roosevelt expected a visitor, he sat up late the night before, reading up on the subject in which he knew his guest was particularly interested. For Roosevelt knew, as all leaders know, that the royal road to a person's heart is to talk about the things he or she treasures most."

PRINCIPLE 6: "Make the Other Person Feel Important and Do It Sincerely—The unvarnished truth is that almost all the people you meet feel superior to you in some way, and a sure way to their hearts is to let them realize in some subtle way that you recognize their importance and recognize it sincerely.

Jesus summed it all up in one thought, probably the most important rule in the world: *'Do to others whatever you would like them to do to you...'*" (Matthew 7:12, NLT).

How to Win People to Your Way of Thinking

PRINCIPLE 1: "You Can't Win an Argument—Nine times out of ten, an argument ends with each of the contestants more firmly convinced than ever that he is absolutely right. The only way to get the best of an argument is to avoid it."

PRINCIPLE 2: "Show Respect for the Other Person's Opinions, Never Say 'You're Wrong.' Nothing good is accomplished, and a lot of damage can be done if you tell a person straight out that he or she is wrong. You only succeed in stripping that person of self-dignity and making yourself an unwelcome part of any discussion."

PRINCIPLE 3: "If You Are Wrong, Admit it Quickly and Emphatically—Any fool can try to defend his or her mistakes, and most fools do. But it raises one above the herd and gives one a feeling of nobility and exultation to admit one's mistakes. When we are right, let's try to win people gently and tactfully to our way of thinking, and when we are wrong, and that will be surprisingly often, if we are honest with ourselves, let's admit our mistakes quickly and with enthusiasm."

PRINCIPLE 4: "Begin in a Friendly Way—The use of gentleness and friendliness is demonstrated day after day by people who have learned that a drop of honey catches more flies than a gallon of gall."

PRINCIPLE 5: "Get the Other Person Saying 'yes, yes' Immediately—In talking with people, don't begin by discussing the things on which you differ. Begin by emphasizing, and keep emphasizing, the things on which you agree. The more 'Yeses' we can, at the very outset induce, the more likely we are to succeed in capturing the attention for our ultimate proposal."

PRINCIPLE 6: "Let the Other Person Do a Great Deal of the Talking—Most people trying to win others to their way of thinking do too much talking themselves. Let the other people talk themselves out. They know more about their business and problems than you do. Letting the other person do the talking helps in family situations as well as in business."

PRINCIPLE 7: "Let the Other Person Feel That the Idea Is His or Hers—No one likes to feel that he or she is being sold something or told to do a thing. We much prefer to feel that we are buying of our own accord or acting on our own ideas. We like to be consulted about our wishes, our wants, our thoughts."

PRINCIPLE 8: "Try Honestly to See Things from the Other Person's Point of View—Remember that other people may be totally wrong, but they don't think so. Don't condemn them. Any fool can do that. Try to understand them. Success in dealing with people depends on a sympathetic grasp of the other person's viewpoint."

PRINCIPLE 9: "Be Sympathetic with the Other Person's Ideas and Desires—Three-fourths of the people you will ever meet are hungering and thirsting for sympathy. Give it to them, and they will love you."

PRINCIPLE 10: "Appeal to the Nobler Motives—A person usually has two reasons for doing something: one that sounds good and a real one. The person himself will think of the real reason. You don't need to emphasize that. But all of us, being idealists at heart, like to think of motives that sound good. So, in order to change people, appeal to the nobler motives."

PRINCIPLE 11: "Dramatize Your Ideas—Merely stating a truth isn't enough. The truth has to be made vivid, interesting, and dramatic. You have to use showmanship. The movies do it, television does it, and you will have to do it if you want attention."

PRINCIPLE 12: "Throw Down a Challenge—The way to get things done is to stimulate competition. I do not mean in a sordid, money-getting way but in the desire to excel. The desire to excel! The challenge! Throwing down the gauntlet! An infallible way of appealing to people of spirit."

Be a Leader: How to Change People Without Giving Offense or Arousing Resentment

PRINCIPLE 1: "Begin with Praise and Honest Appreciation—It is always easier to listen to unpleasant things after we have heard some praise of our good points. Beginning with praise is like a dentist who begins his work with Novocain. The patient still gets a drilling, but the Novocain is painkilling."

PRINCIPLE 2: "Call Attention to People's Mistakes Indirectly—Many people begin their criticism with sincere praise followed by the word 'but' and ending with a critical statement. Simply changing one three-letter word can often spell the difference between failure and success in changing people without giving offense or arousing resentment. This can be easily overcome by changing the word 'but' to 'and.' Instead of: 'We are really proud of you for raising your grades, *but* if you had worked harder, your results would have been even better.' Try: 'We are really proud of you for raising your grades, *and* by continuing to work hard, your grades will get better and better.'"

PRINCIPLE 3: "Talk About Your Own Mistakes Before Criticizing the Other Person—It isn't nearly so difficult to listen to a recital of your faults if the person criticizing begins by humbly admitting that he, too, is far from impeccable. Admitting one's own mistakes, even when one hasn't corrected them, can help convince somebody to change his behavior."

PRINCIPLE 4: "Ask Questions Instead of Giving Direct Orders—No one likes to take orders." When possible, give people the opportunity to share in the decision-making process and let them learn from making their mistakes. "A technique like that saves a person's pride and gives him or her a feeling of importance. It encourages cooperation instead of rebellion. Resentment caused by a brash order may last a long time, even if the order was given to correct an obvious bad situation. Asking questions not only makes an order more palatable; it often stimulates the creativity of the persons whom you ask. People are more likely to accept an order if they have had a part in the decision that caused the order to be issued."

PRINCIPLE 5: "Let the Other Person Save Face—We ride roughshod over the feelings of others, getting our own way, finding fault, issuing threats, criticizing a child or employee in front of others, without even considering the hurt to the other person's pride. Even if we are right and the other person is definitely wrong, we only destroy ego by causing someone to lose face. The legendary French aviation pioneer and author Antoine de Saint-Exupery wrote: 'I have no right to say or do anything that diminishes a man in his own eyes. What matters is not what I think of him but what he thinks of himself. Hurting a man in his dignity is a crime.'"

PRINCIPLE 6: "Spur People on to Success—Let us praise even the slightest improvement. That inspires the other person to keep on improving. When criticism is minimized and praise emphasized, the good things people do will be reinforced, and the poorer things will atrophy for lack of attention. Everybody likes to be praised, but when praise is specific, it comes across as sincere, not something the other person may be saying just to make one feel good. But nobody wants insincerity. Nobody wants flattery."

This is just the tip of the iceberg relative to the wealth of knowledge and wisdom you'll find in Dale Carnegie's book, ***How to Win Friends and Influence People***. I believe this is a book that should absolutely be required reading in our high schools and universities!

Take a Break with Some Humor

I read an article that said the way to achieve inner peace is to finish things I had started. Today, I finished two bags of potato chips, a chocolate pie, and a large bag of M&Ms. I feel better already.

The efficiency expert concluded his lecture with a note of caution. "You don't want to try these techniques at home."

"Why not?" asked someone from the back of the audience.

I watched my wife's routine at breakfast for years," the expert explained. "She made lots of trips to the refrigerator, stove, table, and cabinets, often carrying just a single item at a time. 'Hon,' I suggested, 'Why don't you try carrying several things at once?'"

The voice from the back asked, "Did it save time?"

The expert replied, "Actually, yes. It used to take her twenty minutes to get breakfast ready. Now I do it in seven."

The manager of a large office noticed a new man one day and called him into his office. “What is your name?” was the first thing the manager asked the new guy.

“John,” the new guy replied.

The manager scowled, “Look, I don’t know what kind of soft patsy place you worked at before, but I don’t call anyone by their first name. It breeds familiarity, and that leads to a breakdown in authority. I refer to my employees by their last name only—Smith, Jones, Baker—that’s all. I am to be referred to only as Mr. Robertson. Now that we got that straight, what is your last name?”

The new guy sighed and said, “Darling. John Darling.”

“Okay, John, the next thing I want to tell you is…”

PART 2:
Financial Wisdom

CHAPTER 11:
How to Become a Billionaire

You Have to Start Thinking Like One!

Have you ever wondered why the super-rich keep getting richer, and most everyone else just keeps getting by, or worse yet, in some cases, keeps going backward financially?

For as he thinks in his heart, so is he... (Proverbs 23:7, NKJV).

Scot Anderson, author of *Think Like a Billionaire*, says, "Billionaires think differently than we do. If we took all of a billionaire's money away, in a matter of time, they would be right back to where they are today because of the way they think."

The following words of wisdom are excerpts from Anderson's book.

"Billionaires Think Differently About:

MONEY: We look for ways to spend money. Billionaires look for ways to invest money.

When it comes to money, the wealthy have self-control. This is one of the biggest battles you have to win inside of you. To have self-control, you need vision. Vision brings restraints and boundaries into your life. Without vision, you have no boundaries.

Your vision dictates your outcome. If your vision is big, your outcome will be big. If your vision is small, your outcome will be small.

INVESTING: We invest just a little. Billionaires realize investing is the key to abundance.

JOBS: We think a better job will make us wealthy.

Billionaires know that a job will never make them wealthy; investments will.

RISKS: We stay away from risks because we might fail. Billionaires know if they don't take risks, they've already failed.

Ask any billionaire how he got where he is today, and he will say, 'Risks!' You cannot achieve success without stepping out. We stay average because we play it safe. Billionaires become wealthy because they stepped out and took a chance. We say, 'What if we fail?' Billionaires say, 'You fail if you don't take a risk.'

Most billionaires have had more than three businesses go under. Most billionaires have gone bankrupt at least one time, some multiple times.

Life is full of risks. We face them every day. If you want to have any success in life, you have to be willing to try some things, take a few chances, and step into areas that are new and often unfamiliar to you.

You have to study and learn, but you also have to work and apply what you learn for success to happen.

One of the principles that you have to commit to is becoming a person of action. In life, everything we do that has a reward to it also involves some risk. There is no reward without risk.

Failing at something does not make you a failure unless you stop trying.

PROBLEMS: We try to avoid problems. Billionaires see problems as opportunities to make millions.

Nothing happens in life just because you want it to. You have to make some effort. There will always be obstacles to your progress. But you have to start thinking differently about the problems you face. They cannot be things that cause you to give up. They have to be overcome.

What stands between you and success? You have to identify it and figure out how you are going to conquer it and be successful in whatever you are doing. You must think differently so that you are not intimidated by the obstacles.

Billionaires know that problems are what make life so great. Problems are where millions are made. We ignore problems. Billionaires conquer them. We try to get away from problems. Billionaires go after problems. We want a problem-free life. Billionaires know that problems are what life is about.

Successful people welcome challenges. They look for mountains to climb. The average person tries to find a way around mountains instead of climbing them. They try to circumvent and avoid problems. They try to get away from any negative circumstances in their lives, so they avoid and never face their problems.

If you want to move to the next level, you have to become a problem solver, not a problem avoider. How successful you become in life is based on how you handle problems.

If you are a problem solver on your job, your boss will love you. You will become irreplaceable in his life. He's going to give you raises and promotions and do anything he can to keep you there. Do you want job security? Become a problem solver. There are plenty of problem-finders in every business. Problem solvers are the ones who rise to the top because they are so rare.

Understand this. The more successful you are in life, the more problems you will have.

PREPARATION: We prepare today for today. Billionaires prepare today for the opportunities of tomorrow.

Billionaires know that life is about windows of opportunity. If they are not ready for the window, they will miss the opportunity. People have windows of opportunity open for them all the time. But they usually miss them because they are not prepared. The windows close before they take action.

If you do not prepare for things that will happen in your life, you will go through every single day the same way. You will not grow or change. Billionaires use a portion of time each day to prepare for whatever comes their way tomorrow.

What you want in life will not just drop in your lap. Windows of opportunity will open, and if you are not prepared for them, they will pass you by. The amount of preparation that you do will determine your harvest.

You have to seek wisdom and prepare for the opportunities you want. Knowledge and wisdom will catapult you in your business or whatever you do.

TIME: We waste time. Billionaires see time as their most valuable asset. A billionaire's most valuable asset is not his money. It is not his car, his house, or even his corporation. It is his time. Time is the only limited resource we have. I can get more money. I can get another car. But I can never get more time. My time here on earth is limited.

The successful do not waste their time. They do not let it get away. They maximize every minute and every hour of every day. Time is irreplaceable in your life.

Your time and how you use it now is producing your tomorrow. You have to ask yourself one question. What are you producing? If you do not commit your time to learning how to get where you want to be, you will never go anywhere.

You have to identify your time wasters, and you have to remove them.

Change your mind, and you will change your future. Start today. Tomorrow depends on it."

Now that you know what it's going to take to become a "billionaire" or maybe just a multi-millionaire, Chapter 12 will help you begin the process.

CHAPTER 12:
Get Out of Debt and Start Building Wealth

In the next few chapters, we'll look at the steps necessary to get out of debt, how to become better money managers, and how to begin living a debt-free lifestyle.

The very first step to getting out of debt and building wealth, no matter what age you are or how much money you are making, is *ALWAYS SPEND LESS THAN YOU MAKE* and put what's left in a savings account. It sounds so simple, but many folks find it so hard to do!

According to Larry Burkett, the author of *How to Manage Your Money Workbook*, here are the tell-tale signs of financial bondage:

1. *Overdue Bills* => anxiety, fear, frustration, worry.
2. *Family Needs Unmet* => food, clothing, shelter, medicine.
3. *Greed* => desiring more than what you have or always wanting the best.
4. *Covetousness* => desiring what others have.
5. *A "Get Rich Quick" Attitude* => jumping into an investment or purchase (a) you don't understand, (b) you can't afford, (c) you are being forced to make a hasty decision.
6. *Deceitfulness* => Lying to others for financial gain.
7. *Worry about Investments* => investing money you can't afford to lose.
8. *Laziness* => won't work or unwilling to look for work.
9. *Over-commitment to Work* => Too busy making a living to make a life.

10. *Money Entanglements* => robbing Peter to pay Paul, using credit cards to pay other bills.
11. *Self-Indulgence* => irresponsible spending on items that yield temporary satisfaction and little utility.
12. *Financial Superiority* => pride and hoarding.
13. *Financial Resentment* => blaming others for your financial problems, including God.

Larry Burkett also gives us the steps to freedom from financial bondage:

If you're a Christian, *Transfer Ownership to God* => tithing is the best way to do this. Giving 10 percent of your gross income, or more, to the church you attend is the best way to show God that you are trusting Him to meet all your needs with what is left.

1. *Get Out of Debt and Stay Out* => (a) buy on a cash-only basis, (b) practice saving money regularly.
2. *Refuse Quick Decisions* => wait 30 days before making major purchases or investments. Maybe you'll change your mind!
3. *Excel In Your Work* => Become a valuable asset to your company. If downsizing happens, your value will help keep you off the layoff list.
4. *Contentment* => seek a moderate lifestyle.
5. *Provide for Family Needs* => food, clothing, shelter, medicine.
6. *Balanced Commitment* => God, family, work, leisure time.
7. When necessary, *Sacrifice Wants and Desires* to provide for your needs. (a) *Needs*—purchases necessary to provide for your basic requirements such as food, clothing, shelter, medical coverage, etc. (b) *Wants*—

choices about the quality of goods to be used. (c) *Desires*—choices that can be made only out of surplus funds after all other obligations have been met.

8. *Put Others First* => Jesus said, *"It is more blessed to give than to receive"* (Acts 20:35, NKJV).

It's important to understand that there is a difference between borrowing to make a purchase and *real debt*:

1. Buying something on credit is a *contract* between the lender and the borrower. It is an *agreement* to pay.
2. *Debt* is the *inability* to meet agreed-upon obligations.

A car loan, college loan, home mortgage, etc., doesn't mean you are in debt unless you begin to fall behind and fail to meet your obligations to make scheduled payments on these loans.

Having said that, initiating a money management plan that pays off car loans, college loans, and even home mortgages will bring total financial freedom and allow you to practice greater generosity in other areas of your life.

"We spend January 1 walking through our lives, room by room, drawing up a list of work to be done, cracks to be patched. Maybe this year, to balance the list, we ought to walk through the rooms of our lives... not looking for flaws, but for potential." ~ Ellen Goodman

In Chapter 13, we'll look at the steps necessary to get out of debt.

CHAPTER 13:
Get Out and Stay Out!

Assuming you have more debt than you can handle right now, below are some next steps you can take to begin moving from financial bondage to financial freedom today!

Helpful Hints for Household Expense Reduction & Income Generation

1. IMMEDIATELY STOP USING *ALL* CREDIT CARDS UNLESS IT IS AN *ABSOLUTE EMERGENCY*. Move to a cash-only plan for all household purchases.
2. Assess whether or not additional streams of income are possible and prudent.
   - Consider second or third part-time jobs outside and/or inside your home (home-based businesses: tutoring, selling unneeded items on eBay, Craigslist, Letgo, Marketplace, garage sales, flea markets, home parties, direct mail, etc.)
3. Can you take additional payroll tax deductions without owing Uncle Sam at year-end?
   - If you claim "0" just to get a check back from the IRS for overpaying your taxes, you have just given Uncle Sam an interest-free loan all year long! Why not put that money in your pocket each payday and use it to pay off credit cards or to open a savings account? (see your tax preparer to help determine how many deductions you can legally take.)
   - Make sure you take every tax deduction & tax credit you are entitled to when filing taxes.

4. Homeowners—Do you carry mortgage insurance through your bank? You may qualify to eliminate it. Check it out!
5. Homeowner & Car insurance—When did you last shop for new quotes/lower rates?
6. Life, Health, Disability, Long Term Care Insurance, etc.—When did you last shop for new quotes/lower rates?
7. Eating out? How often? Where? Reduce or eliminate until you are out of debt.
8. Vacations? Scale back or eliminate until you are out of debt.
9. Utilities: Gas/Electricity—Are you on a budget plan to help normalize monthly expenses for better budgeting? Call your provider and ask if they will put you on a budget plan.
10. Telephones/Cell phones/Cable vs. Satellite TV/Internet—Whistles & Bells? Basic plans vs. premium plans. Reassess possible cost reductions.
11. Sanitation—Do you have a choice of provider? Shop around if you can.
12. Groceries: Bulk vs. Prepackaged? Generic vs. Name Brand? A membership to Sam's Club, Costco, etc., might be worth the membership fee for potential savings.
13. Gasoline: How much for your last fill-up? Check around town, call your local radio station, and download the "Gas Guru" app on your cell phone.
14. Expensive leisure activities: golf, bowling, pro sporting events, first-run movies, etc.? Reduce or eliminate until you are out of debt.

15. Clothing/Shoes—Brand names vs. Generic? (Goodwill, Gabriels, Big Lots, Marshalls, TJ Max, Plato's Closet, and other second-hand outlets)
16. Medical Expense alternatives:
    - Check for free or discounted health clinics in your area
    - Generic drugs & vitamins vs. Brand names (prescription & nonprescription)
    - Ask your doctor for samples when he writes you a prescription
    - To save on prescription drugs, try these apps: (GoodRx, SingleCare, BuzzRx, and Drugs.com)
17. Miscellaneous "Wants & Desires" that can be stopped or put on hold until you are debt-free:
    - Tanning
    - Tattoos/Body piercings and associated expenses
    - Fingernail Treatments/Painting
    - Dry cleaning vs. clothing that doesn't require dry cleaning
    - Subscriptions (magazines, book clubs, music clubs, health clubs, etc.)
    - Pets & associated expenses (food, grooming, boarding, veterinarians, etc.)—Wait until you are debt-free unless pets are already part of your family. They deserve proper care, too.
    - Cigarettes, cigars, pipes, chewing tobacco, vaping, etc.
    - Alcoholic beverages
    - Gift Items (Christmas, Easter, birthdays, weddings, graduations, etc.) for family, friends and relatives? Homemade gifts vs. purchases?

- Yard & Home Maintenance—Do it yourself, when possible, vs. paying someone else.
- Proper maintenance on older vehicles rather than turnover every 2–4 years. These days most properly maintained used cars will last ten years or more.
- Buying "good" used cars vs. buying new—Do your research first!

Baby Steps to Becoming Debt-Free

Once you've found ways to reduce household expenses and are generating some additional income, it's time to implement and commit to a plan that will move you to the ultimate goal of a debt-free lifestyle and financial freedom!

1. Your first priority is to open a savings account and begin building your "Emergency Fund." This fund should only be used to purchase items that truly constitute a household "emergency" (furnace, AC, refrigerator, major car repair, tires, etc.) Experts cite various levels for this kind of fund:
   - Some experts say you should have at least $1,000 saved.
   - Others say you should have 3–6 months of your paycheck saved. Obviously, it will take a while to save this much. However, if you should lose your job, can you imagine the peace of mind you'll have knowing you can still meet all your monthly expense obligations until you find employment again?
2. Next, if married, you and your spouse must sit down and develop a reasonable monthly spending plan, better known as a budget. Depending on the budget items you choose to plan on, your household income

minus household expenses should equal no less than zero. If single, have someone you trust to hold you accountable and help you complete your monthly spending plan (budget).

3. Once your Emergency Fund is in place, it's time to start accelerating the payoff of your credit cards using a technique some experts refer to as the "payoff ladder." Here's how it works:
   - Assuming you have more than one credit card, you start with the one with the lowest balance owed, not the highest interest rate. This strategy provides you with the quickest payoff, so you are experiencing a quick win. If you can add any additional money to the minimum balance owed, all the better!
   - Once the first card is paid off, you take the money you were paying on it each month and add it to the minimum monthly amount you are paying on the next card until it is paid off.
   - You keep repeating this method until all your credit cards are paid off. Then, commit to using your cards only if you know you can pay off the amount owed in full each month.
4. When your credit cards are all paid off, you can begin adding some of that newfound money to your monthly auto loan and/or mortgage payment, which will accelerate the payoff of those loans and save a ton of interest!

You are now well on your way to debt-free living with greater peace of mind and, hopefully, more money in your pocket!

CHAPTER 14:
DEBT—The Good, the Bad, and the Ugly

In this chapter, we'll dive a little deeper into the concept of consumer *debt*.

Good Debt vs. Bad Debt

For the sake of this discussion on debt, we're going to assume that all money you owe to anyone is called *debt,* regardless of your ability to repay your loan obligations.

According to Bankrate.com, "When used intelligently, debt can be of tremendous assistance in building wealth. One of the secrets, therefore, to being smart with your money is to differentiate between good debt and bad debt. While the differences often seem logical, it is a logic that apparently is missed by many Americans."

"When you buy something (on credit) that goes down in value immediately, that's bad debt," says David Bach, CEO of Finish Rich Inc. and author of *The Finish Rich Workbook.* "If it has no potential to increase in value, that's bad debt."

Good Debt

"Good debt is investment debt that creates value; for example, student loans, real estate loans, home mortgages, and business loans," says Eric Gelb, CEO of Gateway Financial Advisors and author of *Getting Started in Asset Allocation.* Robert D. Manning, a professor of finance at the Rochester Institute of Technology, also recommends taking on debt that is tax-deductible and debt that produces more wealth in the long run.

These general rules of thumb set some clear delineations—buying a home or refinancing to get rid of excessively high interest rates is usually good debt.

Most financial experts believe that the best type of debt is debt that builds wealth over the long run, and the number one example of that is mortgage debt. "About 40 percent of Americans are renters," says David Bach, "and the fastest way to wealth in America is buying where you live." Bach cites some shocking numbers to back this up, "The average renter has a median net worth of $4,000, and the average homeowner has a median net worth of about $150,000."

Bad Debt

The concept of bad debt comes into play when discussing the purchase of disposable items or durable goods using high-interest credit cards and not paying the balance in full. "The trouble is most people are not organized enough to retire the entire balance before the due date," says Eric Gelb.

Every month that you make a partial payment on your credit account, you are charged interest. The disposable or durable item you purchased continues to lose value, and the amount you paid for it continues to increase. "When you buy clothes, they're probably worth less than 50 percent of what you pay for them when you walk out the door," says David Bach. "So, if you borrowed to pay for them, that's bad debt.

Another bad debt area is auto debt. While most people need an automobile, and the ultimate cost of an auto is higher than many people can pay in one lump sum, the way people go about it—namely, purchasing more car than they need—turns it into bad debt." The moment a new car is purchased and driven off the lot, it loses about 25 percent of its value!

The Ugly Credit Rating Effect

It's also important to understand what that debt could potentially do to your credit rating. "Total personal debt should not exceed 36 percent of your total income," says

Gelb. Keeping the debt-to-income ratio in mind, it's also important not to miss payments. "Missed payments are trouble," he says. "A representative of Citibank said if you don't pay within 30 days, they report that to the credit bureaus."

When it comes to buying durable goods that won't contribute to wealth generation, Bach offers a basic rule of thumb. "My grandma used to say that if you're going to buy something that doesn't go up in value, and you can't afford to pay cash, then you can't afford it."

Exacerbating the bad debt factor is that people will apply for store credit for the savings offers that say, if you open a credit card account today, you can take 10 percent to 20 percent off the cost of your purchase. What people often don't realize is how much of that savings will be destroyed by the high-interest rate on the card if they fail to pay for the items immediately. "You can open a store credit card account," says Bach, "and what they're not telling you is that after the first few months, the rate jumps to 20 percent or greater."

Poor credit ratings due to slow or non-payment of loans and/or credit cards will scare other lenders away from considering your future credit and loan requests. Improving your credit score is a critically important piece of the puzzle when working towards financial freedom. Higher credit scores ensure lower interest rates.

I hope this review on debt was helpful and encourages you to think twice before pulling out those credit cards or signing for a loan without first considering the ramifications of good debt versus bad debt.

Short of buying a house or car, if you can't pay cash for your purchases, or you know you won't be able to pay off your monthly credit card bills in full, then like David Bach's grandma used to say, "You can't afford it!"

I'll admit it's easier said than done, but it's a great first step in working towards a debt-free lifestyle.

CHAPTER 15: Next Steps to Financial Freedom

Once your credit cards are all paid off, your "emergency savings account" is fully funded to a level you are comfortable with, and you are living on a written monthly spending plan (budget), you should be pleasantly surprised at how much money you now have available at the end of each month!

With that extra money available at the end of each month, it's now time to start planning a retirement strategy.

A very important first step you should take as you begin thinking about your retirement plans is to personally assess what kind of investor you are from an emotional perspective. In other words, matching your investment risk tolerance to your personality when it comes to money issues.

Your risk tolerance is your level of comfort with the ups and downs of investing. In order to make the best investment for you as an individual, you will want to find assets that match your risk tolerance.

Low-Risk Tolerance

Are you going to lose sleep whenever your assets decline in value? If so, your risk tolerance is low. Investments that match your risk tolerance profile include basic savings accounts, money market accounts, and certificates of deposit.

Today, these types of accounts will generate returns in the range of 1 to 3 percent annually. Using the Rule of 72, which says 72 divided by the rate of return = the number of years it will take for your money to double one time.

Assuming your best rate of return at 3 percent: 72/3 = 24 years for your stash to double one time! Unfortunately, a very costly and impossible retirement strategy unless you have a BIG bucket of money to start with earning interest at these rates!

Medium-Risk Tolerance

If you don't sweat small declines but do stress over the big ones, your risk tolerance is medium. Investments that match this risk tolerance profile include stocks of large, established, financially healthy companies and mutual funds that balance stock and bond holdings.

Investments in this category might average 4 to 8 percent annually. Assuming your best rate of return at 8 percent: 72/8 = 9 years for your stash to double one time! It's not too bad if you've got a lot of years left before retiring!

High-Risk Tolerance

Those with a high-risk tolerance aren't bothered by market swings as they are only concerned with long-term gains. Those with a high-risk tolerance will likely find their investment matches in sophisticated, higher-risk investments and stocks of hi-tech and startup companies.

Investments in this category might average 9 to 12 percent, more or less, annually. Assuming your best rate of return at 12 percent: 72/12 = 6 years for your stash to double one time!

Adjust Investments as Risk Tolerance Changes

Your risk tolerance will change as your investment goals, financial situation, and life experiences evolve. Generally, the longer the length of time until you need your money, the more risk you can afford to take. In order to make the best investment, consider where you are in life right now.

Risk tolerance is highest for investments you have

chosen to meet faraway goals, such as retirement, because your investments have more time to potentially recover from drops in value.

Conversely, tolerance is lowest for investments to meet short-term goals, such as saving up for educational costs, vacations, and other instances where you will need the money sooner. Especially if your retirement years are approaching fast!

Unless you're a financial wizard and love doing stock market research on what's hot and what's not, it's best to get professional advice from a certified financial planner and/ or someone you feel extremely comfortable entrusting your hard-earned money with.

You can learn to do your own investing, but you also have to be willing to invest the time learning more before you dive in on your own!

A book I wish I had read 30 years ago, *Rule #1*, written by Phil Town, is an excellent book for those who want to learn more, in one book, about personal investing and taking matters into your own hands.

It's not for everyone, but it just might be for you.

Well, I hope this discussion on debt-free living and financial freedom has given you some fresh incentive to make some life-changing decisions with your finances.

Don't let current circumstances overwhelm you! Start today and take baby steps. If you do, I promise you will be pleasantly surprised where you'll be with your financial status come this time next year!

PART 3:
Spiritual Wisdom

CHAPTER 16:
The Wisest Person the World Has Ever Known

The very best place to start this section is, arguably, with the wisest person to ever walk the face of the earth, short of Jesus Christ. His name is King Solomon. He ruled the nation of Israel for 40 years, from 970 to 930 B.C.

Biblical scholars believe Solomon was about twenty years old when his father, Kind David, died, and Solomon was named King of Israel. After Solomon's accession to the throne, he went to Gibeon, the most important high place at that time, to offer sacrifices to God.

"At Gibeon the LORD appeared to Solomon during the night in a dream, and God said, 'Ask for whatever you want me to give you'" (1 Kings 3:5, NIV).

Solomon answered, *"Now, LORD my God, You have made Your servant king in place of my father David. But I am only a little child* (He was young and inexperienced, but he was humble enough to admit it) *and do not know how to carry out my duties"* (1 Kings 3:7, NIV).

Solomon continued, *"So give Your servant a discerning heart to govern Your people and to distinguish between right and wrong. For who is able to govern this great people of Yours?"* (1 Kings 3:9, NIV)

I wonder how each of us would have answered God under the same circumstances, or more realistically, if our boss asked that same question.

Whether we are parents, grandparents, business owners, or in any kind of leadership role, especially as politicians, how I hope we would all ask for the same things Solomon asked for! The wisdom to "distinguish between right and wrong" with those we have power and authority over. And a "discerning heart" with the courage and boldness to do what is right, regardless of personal cost!

"The LORD was pleased that Solomon had asked for this. So God said to him, 'Since you have asked for this and not for long life or wealth for yourself, nor have you asked for the death of your enemies but for discernment in administering justice, I will do what you have asked. I will give you a wise and discerning heart, so that there will never have been anyone like you, nor will there ever be. *Moreover, I will give you what you have not asked for—both riches and honor—so that in your lifetime you will have no equal among kings. And if you walk in ways and obey my statutes and commands as David your father did, I will give you a long life'"* (1 Kings 3:10–14, NIV).

How's that for a blessing far beyond one's wildest dreams and expectations, just for answering in a way that pleased God! There's no telling what blessings might be in store for us when we choose to walk and talk in ways that please God!

"God gave Solomon wisdom and very great insight, and a breadth of understanding as measureless as the sand on the seashore. Solomon's wisdom was greater than the wisdom of all the men of the East, and greater than all the wisdom of Egypt. He was wiser than any other man..." (1 Kings 4:29–31, NIV).

"He spoke three thousand proverbs and his songs numbered a thousand and five" (**1** Kings 4:32, NIV).

"Men of all nations came to listen to Solomon's wisdom, sent by all the kings of the world, who had heard of his wisdom" (1 Kings 4:34, NIV).

We see in this biblical account of King Solomon's life that "all the kings of the world" wanted to hear what he had to say.

With that in mind, we'd certainly be foolish not to explore more deeply some of the wisdom King Solomon left us to consider, meditate on, and apply to our own lives!

CHAPTER 17: Character-Building Wisdom

King Solomon wrote three thousand proverbs as he was guided by God's Holy Spirit. Fear not, I'm only going to share a small portion of the verses from the 31 chapters of the book of Proverbs found in the Holy Bible (All verses are from the NLT—New Living Translation).

If you are familiar with the book of Proverbs, then the verses below will be very familiar and just a brief review for you. However, if you have never read Proverbs, I hope these verses will speak great words of wisdom to your heart and mind and whet your appetite with a desire to read the book of Proverbs in its entirety, and the entire Bible for that matter.

King Solomon's Wisdom for the Ages

Chapter 1: The Purpose and Theme of King Solomon's Proverbs

vs. 1–5: *"These are the proverbs of Solomon, David's son, king of Israel. The purpose of these proverbs is to teach people wisdom and discipline and to help them understand wise sayings. Through these proverbs, people will receive instruction in discipline, good conduct, and doing what is right, just, and fair. These proverbs will make the simple-minded clever. They will give knowledge and purpose to young people. Let those who are wise listen to these proverbs and become even wiser. And let those who understand receive guidance by exploring the depth of meaning in these proverbs."*

vs. 7–8: *"Fear of the LORD is the beginning of knowledge. Only fools despise wisdom and discipline. Listen, my child, to what your father teaches you. Don't neglect your mother's teaching."*

Encouragement to Embrace Wisdom

vs. 10, 15: *"My child, if sinners entice you, turn your back on them. Don't go along with them, my child! Stay far away from their paths."*

Chapter 2:
The Moral Benefits of Wisdom

vs. 1–8: *"My child, listen to me and treasure my instructions. Turn your ear to wisdom and concentrate on understanding. Cry out for insight and understanding. Search for them as you would for lost money or hidden treasure. Then you will understand what it means to fear the LORD, and you will gain knowledge of God. For the LORD grants wisdom! From His mouth come knowledge and understanding. He grants a treasure of common sense to the honest. He is a shield to those who walk with integrity. He guards the paths of the just and protects those who are faithful to Him."*

vs. 9–12: *"Then you will understand what is right and just and fair, and you will know how to find the right course of action every time. For wisdom will enter your heart, and knowledge will fill you with joy. Wise planning will watch over you. Understanding will keep you safe. Wisdom will save you from evil people, from those whose speech is corrupt."*

Chapter 3:

vs. 1–8: *"My child, never forget the things I have taught you. Store my commands in your heart, for they will give you a long and satisfying life. Never let loyalty and kindness get away from you! Wear them like a necklace, and write them deep within your heart. Then, you will find favor with both God and people, and you will gain a good reputation.*

Trust in the LORD with all your heart; do not depend on your own understanding. Seek His will in all you do, and He will direct your paths. Don't be impressed with your own wisdom. Instead, fear the LORD and turn your back on evil. Then you will gain renewed health and vitality."

vs. 11–12: *"My child, don't ignore it when the LORD disciplines you, and don't be discouraged when He corrects you. For the LORD corrects those He loves, just as a father corrects a child in whom he delights."*

vs. 21–23: *"My child, don't lose sight of good planning and insight. Hang on to them, for they fill you with life and bring you honor and respect. They keep you safe on your way and keep your feet from stumbling."*

vs. 27, 28: *"Do not withhold good from those who deserve it when it's in your power to help them. If you can help your neighbor now, don't say, 'Come back tomorrow, and then I'll help you.'"*

vs. 31–33: *"Do not envy violent people; don't copy their ways. Such wicked people are an abomination to the LORD, but He offers his friendship to the godly. The curse of the LORD is on the house of the wicked, but His blessing is on the home of the upright."*

Chapter 4:

vs. 7: *"Getting wisdom is the most important thing you can do! And whatever else you do, get good judgment."*

vs. 23, 24, 27: *"Above all else, guard your heart, for it affects everything you do. Avoid all perverse talk; stay far away from corrupt speech. Don't get sidetracked; keep your feet from following evil."*

Chapter 5:

vs. 21–23: *"For the LORD sees clearly what a man does, examining every path he takes. An evil man is held captive by his own sins; they are ropes that catch and hold him. He will die for lack of self-control; he will be lost because of his incredible folly."*

Chapter 6:

vs. 16–19: *"There are six things the LORD hates—no, seven things He detests: haughty eyes, a lying tongue, hands that kill the innocent, a heart that plots evil, feet that race to do wrong, a false witness who pours out lies, a person who sows discord among brothers."*

Chapter 9:

vs. 9–12: *"Fear of the LORD is the beginning of wisdom. Knowledge of the Holy One results in understanding. Wisdom will multiply your days and add years to your life. If you become wise, you will be the one to benefit. If you scorn wisdom, you will be the one to suffer."*

Chapter 10:

vs. 4, 5: *"Lazy people are soon poor; hard workers get rich. A wise youth works hard all summer; a youth who sleeps away the hour of opportunity brings shame."*

vs. 12: *"Hatred stirs up quarrels, but love covers all offenses."*

Chapter 11:

vs. 1–3: *"The LORD hates cheating, but He delights in honesty. Pride leads to disgrace, but with humility comes wisdom. Good people are guided by their honesty. Treacherous people are destroyed by their dishonesty."*

vs. 24, 25, 27: *"It is possible to give freely and become more wealthy, but those who are stingy will lose everything. The generous prosper and are satisfied; those who refresh others will themselves be refreshed. If you search for good, you will find favor, but if you search for evil, it will find you!"*

vs. 29: *"Those who bring trouble on their families inherit only the wind. The fool will be a servant to the wise."*

Chapter 12:

vs. 1: *"To learn, you must love discipline; it is stupid to hate correction."*

vs. 11, 15, 16: *"Hard work means prosperity; only fools idle away their time. Fools think they need no advice, but the wise listen to others. A fool is quick-tempered, but a wise person stays calm when insulted."*

vs. 19–24: *"Truth stands the test of time; lies are soon exposed. Deceit fills hearts that are planning evil; joy fills hearts that are planning peace! No real harm befalls the godly, but the wicked have their fill of trouble. The LORD hates those who don't keep their word, but He delights in those who do. Wise people don't make a show of their knowledge, but fools broadcast their folly. Work hard and become a leader; be lazy and become a slave."*

Chapter 13:

vs. 1, 3, 4: *"A wise child accepts a parent's discipline; a young mocker refuses to listen. Those who control their tongue will have a long life. A quick retort can ruin everything. Lazy people want much but get little, but those who work hard will prosper and be satisfied."*

vs. 10, 11, 13: *"Pride leads to arguments; those who take advice are wise. Wealth from get-rich schemes quickly disappears; wealth from hard work grows. People who despise advice will find themselves in trouble; those who respect it will succeed."*

vs. 21, 24: *"Trouble chases sinners, while blessings chase the righteous. If you refuse to discipline your children, it proves you don't love them; if you love your children, you will be prompt to discipline them."*

Chapter 14:

vs. 2, 26: *"Those who follow the right path fear the LORD; those who take the wrong path despise Him. Those who fear the LORD are secure; He will be a place of refuge for their children."*

vs. 29–31: *"Those who control their anger have great understanding; those with a hasty temper will make mistakes. A relaxed attitude lengthens life; jealousy rots it away. Those who oppress the poor insult their Maker, but those who help the poor honor Him."*

Chapter 15:

vs. 1, 2, 5: *"A gentle answer turns away wrath, but harsh words stir up anger. The wise person makes learning a joy; fools spout only foolishness. Only a fool despises a parent's discipline; whoever learns from correction is wise."*

vs. 14, 19, 22: *"A wise person is hungry for the truth, while the fool feeds on trash. A lazy person has trouble all through life; the path of the upright is easy! Plans go wrong for lack of advice; many counselors bring success."*

vs. 29, 31–33: *"The LORD is far from the wicked, but He hears the prayers of the righteous. If you listen to constructive criticism, you will be at home among the wise. If you reject criticism, you only harm yourself, but if you listen to correction, you grow in understanding. Fear of the LORD teaches a person to be wise; humility precedes honor."*

Chapter 16:

vs. 2, 3, 9: *"People may be pure in their own eyes, but the LORD examines their motives. Commit your work to the LORD, and then your plans will succeed. We can make our plans, but the LORD determines our steps."*

vs. 18: *"Pride goes before destruction, and haughtiness before a fall."*

Chapter 17:

vs. 3, 5: *"Fire tests the purity of silver and gold, but the LORD tests the heart. Those who mock the poor insult their Maker; those who rejoice at the misfortune of others will be punished."*

vs. 9, 13: *"Disregarding another person's faults preserves love; telling about them separates close friends. If you repay evil for good, evil will never leave your house."*

vs. 18, 27: *"It is poor judgment to co-sign a friend's note, to become responsible for a neighbor's debts. A truly wise person uses few words; a person with understanding is even-tempered."*

Chapter 18:

vs. 2, 4: *"Fools have no interest in understanding; they only want to air their own opinions. A person's words can be life-giving-water; words of true wisdom are as refreshing as a bubbling brook."*

vs. 9, 15: *"A lazy person is as bad as someone who destroys things. Intelligent people are always open to new ideas. In fact, they look for them."*

vs. 22: *"The man who finds a wife finds a treasure and receives favor from the LORD."*

Chapter 19:

vs. 2, 3: *"Zeal without knowledge is not good; a person who moves too quickly may go the wrong way. People ruin their lives by their own foolishness and then are angry at the LORD."*

vs. 8, 9: *"To acquire wisdom is to love oneself; people who cherish understanding will prosper. A false witness will not go unpunished, and a liar will be destroyed."*

vs. 11, 17, 18: *"People with good sense restrain their anger; they earn esteem by overlooking wrongs. If you help the poor, you are lending to the LORD—and He will repay you! Discipline your children while there is hope. If you don't, you will ruin their lives."*

Chapter 20:

vs. 1, 3: *"Wine produces mockers; liquor leads to brawls. Whoever is led astray by drink cannot be wise. Avoiding a fight is a mark of honor; only fools insist on quarreling."*

vs. 7, 11: *"The godly walk with integrity; blessed are their children after them. Even children are known by the way they act, whether their conduct is pure and right."*

vs. 18, 19: *"Plans succeed through good counsel; don't go to war without the advice of others.*

A gossip tells secrets, so don't hang around with someone who talks too much."

Chapter 21:

vs. 2, 5: *"People may think they are doing what is right, but the LORD examines the heart. Good planning and hard work lead to prosperity, but hasty shortcuts lead to poverty."*

vs. 13: *"Those who shut their ears to the cries of the poor will be ignored in their own time of need."*

vs. 20, 25, 30: *"The wise have wealth and luxury, but fools spend whatever they get. The desires of lazy people will be their ruin, for their hands refuse to work. They are always greedy for more, while the godly love to give!"*

Chapter 22:

vs. 1–3: *"Choose a good reputation over great riches, for being held in high esteem is better than having silver and gold. The rich and the poor have this in common: The LORD made them both. A prudent person foresees the danger ahead and takes precautions; the simpleton goes blindly on and suffers the consequences."*

vs. 6, 15: *"Teach your children to choose the right path, and when they are older, they will remain upon it. A youngster's heart is filled with foolishness, but discipline will drive it away."*

Chapter 23:

vs. 4, 12, 17: *"Don't weary yourself trying to get rich. Why waste your time? For riches can disappear as though they had the wings of a bird! Commit yourself to instruction; attune your ears to hear words of knowledge. Don't envy sinners, but always continue to fear the LORD."*

vs. 20: *"Do not carouse with drunkards and gluttons, for they are on their way to poverty. Too much sleep clothes a person with rags."*

Chapter 24:

vs. 1, 5, 6: *"Don't envy evil people; don't desire their company. A wise man is mightier than a strong man, and a man of knowledge is more powerful than a strong man. So don't go to war without wise guidance; victory depends on having many counselors."*

vs. 11, 12: *"Rescue those who are unjustly sentenced to death; don't stand back and let them die. Don't try to avoid responsibility by saying you didn't know about it. For God knows all hearts, and He sees you. He keeps watch over your soul, and He knows you knew! And He will judge all people according to what they have done."*

vs. 17, 18: *"Do not rejoice when your enemies fall into trouble. Don't be happy when they stumble. For the LORD will be displeased with you and will turn His anger away from them."*

vs. 27: *"Develop your business first before building your house."*

Chapter 25:

vs. 12, 15: *"Valid criticism is as treasured by the one who heeds it as jewelry made from finest gold. Patience can persuade a prince, and soft speech can crush strong opposition."*

vs. 28: *"A person without self-control is as defenseless as a city with broken-down walls."*

Chapter 26:

vs. 17–20: *"Yanking a dog's ear is as foolish as interfering in someone else's argument. Just as damaging as a madman shooting a lethal weapon is someone who lies to a friend and then says, 'I was only joking.' Fire goes out for lack of fuel, and quarrels disappear when gossip stops."*

vs. 24–26: *"People with hate in their hearts may sound pleasant enough, but don't believe them. Though they pretend to be kind, their hearts are full of all kinds of evil. While their hatred may be concealed by trickery, it will finally come to light for all to see."*

Chapter 27:

vs. 1, 2: *"Don't brag about tomorrow since you don't know what the day will bring. Don't praise yourself; let others do it!"*

vs. 12, 17: *"A prudent person foresees the danger ahead and takes precautions. The simpleton goes blindly on and suffers the consequences. As iron sharpens iron, a friend sharpens a friend."*

Chapter 28:

vs. 9, 13: *"The prayers of a person who ignores the law are despised. People who cover their sins will not prosper. But if they confess and forsake them, they will receive mercy."*

vs. 20, 22: *"The trustworthy will get a rich reward. But the person who wants to get rich quick will only get into trouble. A greedy person tries to get rich quick, but it only leads to poverty."*

vs. 27: *"Whoever gives to the poor will lack nothing. But a curse will come upon those who close their eyes to poverty."*

Chapter 29:

vs. 1, 11: *"Whoever stubbornly refuses to accept criticism will suddenly be broken beyond repair. A fool gives full vent to anger, but a wise person quietly holds it back."*

vs. 15, 17: *"To discipline and reprimand a child produces wisdom, but a mother is disgraced by an undisciplined child. Discipline your children, and they will give you happiness and peace of mind."*

vs. 20, 22, 23: *"There is more hope for a fool than for someone who speaks without thinking. A hot-tempered person starts fights and gets into all kinds of sin. Pride ends in humiliation, while humility brings honor."*

vs. 25, 27: *"Fearing people is a dangerous trap, but to trust the LORD means safety. The godly despise the wicked; the wicked despise the godly."*

CHAPTER 18: Living with Purpose and Peace

In this chapter, which has six parts, we are going to soak in wisdom from a book that impacted my life immeasurably. It's a Christian-oriented book, a book that expresses the belief in a Creator God and that *every* man and woman is created in His image. Whether or not you believe this, there is a great deal of wisdom in this book for everyone living with purpose and for everyone desiring to live a life filled with purpose and meaning.

The book I'm referring to is *The Purpose Driven Life*, written by Rick Warren, who was the founder and lead pastor at Saddleback Church in Orange County, CA, when he wrote it.

This is a book I try to reread every year whether I need to or not!

Part 1—What on Earth Am I Here For?

Chapter 1. "It All Starts with God: The purpose of your life is far greater than your own personal fulfillment, your peace of mind, or even your happiness. It's far greater than your family, your career, or even your wildest dreams and ambitions. If you want to know why you were placed on this planet, you must begin with God. You were born *by* His purpose and *for* His purpose. You didn't create yourself, so there is no way you can tell yourself what you were created for!"

Chapter 2. "You Are Not an Accident: Your parents may not have planned for you, but God did. God prescribed every detail of your body. He deliberately chose your race, the color of your skin, your hair, and every other feature. He also determined the natural talents you would possess and the uniqueness of your personality. Because God made you for a reason, He also decided *when* you would be born and *how long* you would live."

Chapter 3. "What Drives Your Life?

1. Many people are driven by guilt: Guilt-driven people are manipulated by memories. They allow their past to control their future.
2. Many people are driven by resentment and anger: Instead of releasing their pain through forgiveness, they rehearse it over and over in their minds.
3. Many people are driven by fear: Fear-driven people often miss great opportunities because they're afraid to venture out.
4. Many people are driven by materialism: This drive to always want more is based on the misconception that having more will make me more happy, more important, and more secure, but all three ideas are untrue. Possessions only provide *temporary* happiness.
5. Many people are driven by the need for approval: Being controlled by the opinions of others is a guaranteed way to miss God's purposes for your life."

Chapter 4. "Made to Last Forever: You have an inborn instinct that longs for immortality. This is because God designed you, in His image, to live for eternity. The reason we feel we should live forever is that God wired our brains with that desire! While life on Earth offers many choices, eternity offers only two: Heaven or Hell. Your relationship to God on earth will determine your relationship to Him in eternity."

Chapter 5. "Seeing Life from God's View: The way you see your life *shapes* your life. How you define life determines your destiny. Your perspective will influence how you invest your time, spend your money, use your talents, and value your relationships.

God's view of life: Life is a *test*, life is a *trust*, and life is a *temporary assignment*. God continually tests people's character, faith, obedience, love, integrity, and loyalty. When you understand that life is a test, you realize that nothing is insignificant in your life. Even the smallest incident has significance for your character development."

"Sow a thought, reap an action; sow an action, reap a habit; sow a habit, reap a character; sow a character, reap a destiny!" —Pastor Alistair Begg

"Our time on earth and our energy, intelligence, opportunities, relationships, and resources are all gifts from God that He has entrusted to our care and management. Everything we enjoy is to be treated as a *trust* that God has placed in our hands. Our culture says, 'If you don't own it, you won't take care of it.' But Christians live by a higher standard; 'Because God owns it, I must take the best care of it that I can.' At the end of your life on earth, you will be evaluated and rewarded according to how well you handled what God entrusted to you."

Chapter 6. "Life Is a Temporary Assignment: To make the best use of your life, you must never forget two truths: First, compared with eternity, life is extremely brief. Second, the earth is only a temporary residence. You won't be here long, so don't get too attached. In order to keep us from becoming too attached to the earth, God allows us to feel a significant amount of discontent and dissatisfaction in life—longings that will never be fulfilled on this side of eternity. We're not completely happy here because we're not supposed to be!"

Chapter 7. "The Reason for Everything: Everything created by God reflects His glory in some way. God's five purposes for your life:

1. We bring God glory by worshiping Him

2. We bring God glory by loving other believers
3. We bring God glory by becoming like Christ
4. We bring God glory by serving others with our gifts
5. We bring God glory by telling others about Him

Living the rest of your life for the glory of God will require a change in your priorities, your schedule, your relationships, and everything else. It will sometimes mean choosing a difficult path instead of an easy one."

Part 2 - You Were Planned for God's Pleasure

Chapter 8. "Planned for God's Pleasure: God did not *need* to create you, but He *chose* to create you for his own enjoyment. Bringing enjoyment to God, living for His pleasure, is the first purpose of your life. Bringing pleasure to God is called 'worship.' Anything you do that brings pleasure to God is an act of worship. If we fail to worship God, we always find a substitute, even if it ends up being ourselves. Every activity can be transformed into an act of worship when you do it for the praise, glory, and pleasure of God."

Chapter 9. "What Makes God Smile: The smile of God is the goal of your life. Since pleasing God is the first purpose of your life, your most important task is to discover how to do that.

There are five acts of worship that make God smile.

1. God smiles when we love Him supremely. He longs for you to know Him and spend time with Him. This is why learning to love God and to be loved by Him should be the greatest objective of your life.

2. God smiles when we trust Him completely. Trusting God completely means having faith that He knows what is best for your life.

God smiles when we obey Him wholeheartedly. God

doesn't owe you an explanation or reason for everything He asks you to do. Understanding can wait, but obedience can't. In fact, you will never understand some commands until you obey them first. Obedience unlocks understanding.

God smiles when we praise and thank Him. He smiles when we express our adoration and gratitude to Him.

God smiles when we use our abilities. You don't bring glory or pleasure to God by hiding your abilities or by trying to be someone else. Anytime you reject any part of yourself, you are rejecting God's wisdom and sovereignty in creating you. What God looks at is the attitude of your heart: Is pleasing Him your deepest desire?"

Chapter 10. "The Heart of Worship: The heart of worship is surrender. You know you're surrendered to God when you rely on God to work things out instead of trying to manipulate others, force your agenda, and control the situation. Instead of trying harder, you trust more. You also know you're surrendered when you don't react to criticism and rush to defend yourself."

Chapter 11. "Becoming Best Friends with God: God wants to be your best friend. You will never grow a close relationship with God by just attending church once a week or even having a daily quiet time. Friendship with God is built by sharing *all* your life experiences with Him. *Everything* you do can be 'spending time with God' if He is invited to be a part of it and you stay aware of His presence. Prayer lets you speak to God; meditation lets God speak to you. Both are essential to becoming a friend of God."

Chapter 12. "Developing Your Friendship with God: You are as close to God as you choose to be. Like any friendship, you must work at developing your friendship with God. It won't happen by accident. It takes desire, time, and energy. To achieve friendship with God:

- I must choose to be honest with God. The first building block of a deeper friendship with God is honesty about your faults and your feelings.
- I must choose to obey God in faith. Every time you trust God's wisdom and do whatever he says, even when you don't understand it, you deepen your friendship with God.
- I must choose to value what God values. This is what friends do, they care about what is important to the other person. The more you become God's friend, the more you will care about the things He cares about, grieve over the things He grieves over, and rejoice over the things that bring pleasure to Him.
- I must desire friendship with God more than anything else. The truth is—you are as close to God *as you choose to be*. Intimate friendship with God is a choice, not an accident. You must intentionally seek it."

Chapter 13. "Worship That Pleases God: God doesn't want a part of your life. He asks for *all* of your heart, *all* of your soul, *all* of your mind, and *all* of your strength. The kind of worship that pleases God has four characteristics:

1. God is pleased when our worship is accurate. But we cannot just create our own comfortable or politically correct image of God and worship it. That is idolatry. Worship must be based on the truth of Scripture, not our opinions about God.
2. God is pleased when our worship is authentic. Worship must be genuine and heartfelt. It is not a matter of saying the right words; you must mean what you say. Heartless praise is not praise at all! It is worthless, an insult to God.

3. God is pleased when our worship is thoughtful. I worship is mindless. It is meaningless. You must engage your mind.
4. God is pleased when our worship is practical. One thing worship costs us is our self-centeredness. You cannot exalt God and yourself at the same time. You don't worship to be seen by others or to please yourself. You deliberately shift the focus off yourself."

Chapter 14. "When God Seems Distant: God is real, no matter how you feel. The deepest level of worship is praising God in spite of pain, thanking God during trial, trusting Him when tempted, surrendering while suffering, and loving Him when he seems distant.

When God seems distant, you may feel that He is angry with you or is disciplining you for some sin. In fact, sin *does* disconnect us from intimate fellowship with God. During times of spiritual dryness, you must patiently rely on the promises of God, not your emotions, and realize that He is taking you to a deeper level of maturity. So don't be troubled by trouble. Circumstances cannot change the character of God. When you feel abandoned by God yet continue to trust Him in spite of your feelings, you worship Him in the deepest way."

Part 3 - You Were Formed for God's Family

Chapter 15. "Formed for God's Family: Because God is love, He treasures relationships. His very nature is relational, and He identifies Himself in family terms: Father, Son, and Spirit. The Trinity is God's relationship to Himself. When we place our faith in Christ, God becomes our Father, we become His children, other believers become our brothers and sisters, and the church becomes our spiritual family.

Every human being was *created* by God, but not everyone

is a *child* of God. The only way to get into God's family is by being born again into it. The invitation to be part of God's family is universal, but there is one condition: faith in Jesus. Being included in God's family is the highest honor and the greatest privilege you will ever receive. Nothing else comes close. Whenever you feel unimportant, unloved, or insecure, remember to whom you belong."

Chapter 16. "What Matters Most: Life is about love. Because God is love, the most important lesson He wants you to learn on earth is how to love. It is in loving that we are most like Him, so love is the foundation of every command He has given us. God wants you to be in regular, close fellowship with other believers so you can develop the skill of loving. Love cannot be learned in isolation. You have to be around people—irritating, imperfect, frustrating people. Through fellowship, we learn three important truths.

1. *Life without love is really worthless.* The point of life is learning to love—God and people. Life minus love equals zero.
2. *Love will last forever.* Love leaves a legacy. How you treat other people, not your wealth or accomplishments, is the most enduring impact you can leave on earth. Love is the secret of a lasting heritage.
3. *We will be evaluated on our love.* One of the ways God measures spiritual maturity is by the quality of your relationships.

The most desired gift of love is not diamonds or roses or chocolate. It is *focused attention.* Whenever you give your time, you are making a sacrifice, and sacrifice is the essence of love. Why is now the best time to express love? Because you don't know how long you will have the opportunity. You have no guarantee of tomorrow."

Chapter 17. "A Place to Belong: While your relationship

to Christ is personal, God never intends it to be private. Following Christ includes *belonging*, not just believing. We are *members* of His Body—the church. The church is a body, not a building, an organism, not an organization. Why you need a church family:

- *A church family identifies you as a genuine believer.* When we come together in love as a church family from different backgrounds, races, and social statuses, it is a powerful witness to the world.
- *A church family moves you out of self-centered isolation.* The local church is the classroom for learning how to get along in God's family. It is a lab for practicing unselfish, sympathetic love.
- *A church family helps you develop spiritual muscle.* You will never grow to maturity just by attending worship services and being a passive spectator. Only participation in the full life of a local church builds spiritual muscle.
- *A church family will help keep you from backsliding.* None of us is immune to temptation. Given the right situation, you and I are capable of any sin.

You can spend a lifetime searching for the perfect church, but you will never find it. You are called to love imperfect sinners, just as God does."

Chapter 18. "Experiencing Life Together: Life is meant to be shared. The Bible calls this shared experience *fellowship.* Real fellowship is so much more than just showing up at services. It is *experiencing life together.*

- *In real fellowship, people experience mutuality.* Mutuality is the art of giving and receiving. It's depending on each other. Mutuality is the heart of fellowship.

- *In real fellowship, people experience sympathy.* Sympathy is not giving advice or offering quick, cosmetic help; sympathy is entering in and sharing the pain of others.
- *In real fellowship, people experience mercy.* Fellowship is a place of grace where mistakes aren't rubbed in but rubbed out. Fellowship happens when mercy wins over justice.

You can't have fellowship without forgiveness. Many people are reluctant to show mercy because they don't understand the difference between trust and forgiveness. Forgiveness is letting go of the past. Trust has to do with future behavior. Forgiveness must be immediate, whether or not a person asks for it. Trust must be rebuilt over time."

Chapter 19. "Cultivating Community:

- *Cultivating community takes honesty.* You will have to care enough to lovingly speak the truth, even when you would rather gloss over a problem or ignore an issue.
- *Cultivating community takes humility.* Self-importance, smugness, and stubborn pride destroy fellowship faster than anything else. Humility is the oil that smooths and soothes relationships.
- *Cultivating community takes courtesy.* Courtesy is respecting our differences, being considerate of each other's feelings, and being patient with people who irritate us.
- *Cultivating community takes confidentiality.* Only in the safe environment of warm acceptance and trusted confidentiality will people open up and share their deepest hurts, needs, and mistakes.
- *Cultivating community takes frequency.* You

> *must* have frequent, regular contact with your group in order to build genuine fellowship."

Chapter 20. "Restoring Broken Fellowship: Here are seven biblical steps to restoring fellowship:

1. Talk to God before talking to the person.
2. Always take the initiative.
3. Sympathize with their feelings.
4. Confess your part of the conflict.
5. Attack the problem, not the person.
6. Cooperate as much as possible.
7. Emphasize reconciliation, not resolution."

Chapter 21. "Protecting Your Church: It is your job to protect the unity of your church. Unity is the soul of fellowship. Destroy it, and you rip the heart out of Christ's Body. The Bible gives us practical advice on how to protect the unity of the church.

- Focus on what we have in common, not our differences.
- Be realistic in your expectations.
- Choose to encourage rather than criticize.
- Refuse to listen to gossip.
- Practice God's method of conflict resolution (Matthew 18:15–17a).
- Support your pastor and leaders."

Part 4—You Were Created to Become Like Christ

Chapter 22. "Created to Become Like Christ: From the very beginning, God's plan has been to make you like His Son, Jesus. This is your destiny and the third purpose of your life. In all creation, only human beings are made 'in God's image.'

Like God, we are *spiritual beings*—our spirits are immortal and will outlast our earthly bodies; we are *intellectual*—we can think, reason, and solve problems; like God, we are *relational*—we can give and receive real love, and we have a *moral consciousness*—we can discern right from wrong, which makes us accountable to God.

God's ultimate goal for your life on earth is not comfort but character development. Becoming like Christ does not mean losing your personality or becoming a mindless clone. Christlikeness is all about transforming your character, not your personality. First, we must choose to let go of old ways of acting. Second, we must change the way we think. Third, we must 'put on' the character of Christ by developing new, godly habits. Your character is essentially the sum of your habits; it is how you *habitually* act."

Chapter 23. "How We Grow: Spiritual growth is not automatic. It takes an intentional commitment. You must *want* to grow, *decide* to grow, *make an effort* to grow, and *persist* in growing. Nothing shapes your life more than the commitments you choose to make. Your commitments can develop you, or they can destroy you, but either way, they will define you. We become whatever we are committed to. Your first step in spiritual growth is to start changing the way you think. Change always starts in the mind. The way you *think* determines the way you *feel*, and the way you feel influences the way you *act*. The Christian life is far more than creeds and convictions; it includes conduct and character. Our deeds must be consistent with our creeds, and our beliefs must be backed up with Christlike behavior."

Chapter 24. "Transformed by Truth: God's Word (the Bible) is the spiritual nourishment you *must* have to fulfill your purpose. In day-to-day living, abiding in God's Word includes three activities.

1. *I must accept its authority*. The most important decision you can make today is to settle this issue of what will be the ultimate authority for your life.
2. *I must assimilate its truth.* It is not enough just to believe the Bible; I must fill my mind with it so that the Holy Spirit can transform me with the truth.
3. *I must apply its principles.* This is the hardest step of all because Satan fights it so intensely. He doesn't mind you going to Bible studies as long as you don't do anything with what you learn. We fool ourselves when we assume that just because we have heard, read, or studied a truth, we have internalized it.

As D. L. Moody said, 'The Bible was not given to increase our knowledge but to change our lives.'"

Chapter 25. "Transformed by Trouble: God has a purpose behind every problem. He uses circumstances to develop our character. Jesus warned us that we would have problems in the world. No one is immune to pain or insulated from suffering, and no one gets to skate through life problem-free.

God uses problems to draw you closer to Himself. We learn things about God in suffering that we can't learn any other way. Problems force us to look to God and depend on Him instead of ourselves. Regardless of the cause, none of your problems could happen without God's permission. Because God is sovereignly in control, accidents are just incidents in God's good plan for you. Because every day of your life was written on God's calendar before you were born, *everything* that happens to you has spiritual significance."

Chapter 26. "Growing Through Temptation: Every temptation is an opportunity to do good. On the path to spiritual maturity, even temptation becomes a stepping-stone rather than a stumbling block when you realize that it is just as much an occasion to do the right thing as it is to do the wrong thing. Temptation simply provides the choice. While temptation is Satan's primary weapon to destroy you, God wants to use it to develop you. Every time you choose to do good instead of sin, you are growing in the character of Christ. All temptation follows the same pattern.

- In step one, Satan identifies a *desire* inside of you. Temptation starts when Satan suggests (with a thought) that you give in to an evil desire or that you fulfill a legitimate desire in the wrong way or at the wrong time. Always beware of shortcuts. They are often temptations! Temptation always starts in your mind, not in circumstances.
- Step two is *doubt*. Satan tries to get you to doubt what God has said about the sin.
- Step three is *deception.* Satan is incapable of telling the truth and is called *'the Father of lies.'* Anything he tells you will be untrue or just half true.
- Step four is *disobedience.* You finally act on the thought you've been toying with in your mind. What began as an idea gets birthed into behavior.

Understanding how temptation works is in itself helpful, but there are specific steps you need to take to overcome it.

- *Refuse to be intimidated.* It is not a sin to be tempted. You can't keep the Devil from suggesting thoughts, but you *can* choose not to dwell or act on them.

- *Recognize your pattern of temptation and be prepared for it.* There are certain situations that make you more vulnerable to temptation than others.
- These situations are unique to your weaknesses, and you need to identify them because Satan surely knows them!
- *Request God's help.* Ask Him for the power to do the right thing and then expect Him to provide it."

Chapter 27. "Defeating Temptation: You may sometimes feel that a temptation is too overpowering for you to bear, but that's a lie from Satan. God has promised never to allow more *on* you than He puts *within* you to handle it. He will not permit any temptation that you could not overcome. However, you must do your part, too, by practicing the four biblical keys of defeating temptation.

1. Refocus your attention on something else.
2. Reveal your struggle to a godly friend or support group.
3. Resist the Devil.
4. Realize your vulnerability."

Chapter 28. "It Takes Time: There are no shortcuts to maturity. Before Christ invades our lives at conversion, He sometimes has to 'soften us up' by allowing problems we can't handle. Why does it take so long to change and grow up? There are several reasons.

- We are slow learners.
- We have a lot to unlearn.
- We are afraid to humbly face the truth about ourselves.
- Growth is often painful and scary.
- Habits take time to develop.

There is only one way to develop the habits of Christlike character. You must *practice* them—and that takes time!"

Part 5 - You Were Shaped for Serving God

Chapter 29. "Accepting Your Assignment: You were put on earth to make a contribution. You weren't created just to consume resources. God designed you to make a difference in your life. God wants you to give something back. This is God's fourth purpose for your life, and it is called your 'ministry' or service.

- *You were created to serve God.* Whenever you serve others in any way, you are actually serving God.
- *You were saved to serve God.* You're not saved *by* service, but you are saved *for* service. We are saved to serve, not to sit around and wait for heaven.
- *You are called to serve God.* Your call to salvation includes your call to service. Anytime you use your God-given abilities to help others, you are fulfilling your calling.
- *You are commanded to serve God.* Jesus was unmistakable: *'For even the Son of Man came not to be served but to serve others and to give his life as a ransom for many'* (Matthew 20:28, NLT).

You are going to give your life for something. What will it be—a career, a sport, a hobby, fame, wealth? None of these will have lasting significance. Service is the pathway to real significance. It is through ministry that we discover the meaning of our lives."

Chapter 30. "Shaped for Serving God: Each of us was uniquely designed, or 'shaped,' to do certain things. Before God created you, He decided what role He wanted you to play on earth. Whenever God gives us an assignment, He always equips us with what we need to accomplish it. This custom combination of capabilities is called your *SHAPE:*

Spiritual gifts, Heart, Abilities, Personality, Experience

Unwrapping Your *Spiritual Gifts*: God gives every believer spiritual gifts to be used in ministry. These are special God-empowered abilities for serving Him that are given only to believers. Your spiritual gifts were not given for your own benefit but for the benefit of *others*, just as other people were given gifts for your benefit.

Listening to Your *Heart*: The Bible uses the term *heart* to describe the bundle of desires, hopes, interests, ambitions, dreams, and affections you have. Your heart represents the source of all your motivations—what you love to do and what you care about most. Your heart reveals the *real* you—what you truly are, not what others *think* you are or what circumstances force you to be. Your heart determines why you *say* the things you do, why you *feel* the way you do, and why you *act* the way you do."

Chapter 31. "Understanding Your SHAPE: God designed each of us so there would be no duplication in the world.

Applying Your *Abilities:* Your abilities are the natural talents you were born with. All of our abilities come from God. Even abilities used to sin are God-given; they are just being misused or abused. To discover God's will for your life, you should seriously examine what you are good at doing and what you're not good at. God will never ask you to dedicate your life to a task you have no talent for. On the other hand, the abilities you *do* have are a strong indication of what God wants you to do with your life.

Using Your *Personality*: When God made you, he broke

the mold. There never has been, and never will be, anybody exactly like you. Your personality will affect *how* and *where* you use your spiritual gifts and abilities.

Employing Your *Experiences*: You have been shaped by your experiences in life, most of which were beyond your control. God allowed them for His purpose of molding you. In determining your *SHAPE* for serving God, you should examine at least six kinds of experiences from your past:

1. *Family* experiences: What did you learn growing up in your family?
2. *Educational* experiences: What were your favorite subjects in school?
3. *Vocational* experiences: What jobs have you been most effective in and enjoyed most?
4. *Spiritual* experiences: What have been your most meaningful times with God?
5. *Ministry* experiences: How have you served God in the past?
6. *Painful* experiences: What problems, hurts, thorns, and trials have you learned from?

Using your *SHAPE* is the secret to both fruitfulness and fulfillment in ministry."

Chapter 32. "Using What God Gave You: Begin by assessing your gifts and abilities. Take a long, honest look at what you are good at and what you're not good at. The best way to discover your gifts and abilities is to *experiment* with different areas of service.

Consider your heart and your personality. Ask yourself questions: What do I really enjoy doing most? When do I feel the most fully alive? What am I doing when I lose track of time? Do I like routine or variety? Do I prefer serving with a team or by myself? Am I more introverted or extroverted?

Am I more of a thinker or a feeler? Which do I enjoy more---competing or cooperating?

Your *SHAPE* was sovereignly determined by God for *His* purpose, so you shouldn't resent it or reject it. Instead of trying to reshape yourself to be like someone else, you should celebrate the shape God has given only you."

Chapter 33. "How Real Servants Act: How can you know if you have the heart of a servant?

- *Real servants make themselves available to serve.* Being a servant means giving up the right to control your schedule and allowing God to interrupt it whenever He needs to.
- *Real servants pay attention to needs.* Servants are always on the lookout for ways to help others.
- *Real servants do their best with what they have.* Servants don't make excuses, procrastinate, or wait for better circumstances. They just do what needs to be done.
- *Real servants do every task with equal dedication.* Whatever they do, servants *'do it with all their heart.'* The size of the task is irrelevant. The only issue is, does it need to be done?
- *Real servants are faithful to their ministry.* Servants finish their tasks, fulfill their responsibilities, keep their promises, and complete their commitments.
- They don't leave a job half undone, and they don't quit when they get discouraged. They are trustworthy and dependable.
- *Real servants maintain a low profile.* Servants don't promote or call attention to themselves. Instead of acting to impress and dressing for

> success, they *'put on the apron of humility, to serve one another.'"*

Chapter 34. "Thinking Like a Servant: Service starts in your mind. To be a servant requires a mental shift, a change in your attitude. God is always more interested in *why* we do something than in *what* we do. Attitudes count more than achievements. Real servants serve God with a mindset of five attitudes.

1. *Servants think more about others than about themselves.* This is true humility: not thinking less of ourselves but thinking of ourselves *less*.
2. *Servants think like stewards, not owners.* Servants remember that God owns it all.
3. *Servants think about their work, not what others are doing.* Real servants don't complain of unfairness, don't have pity parties, and don't resent those not serving.
4. *Servants base their identity in Christ.* Because they remember they are loved and accepted by grace, servants don't have to prove their worth. They willingly accept jobs that insecure people would consider 'beneath' them.
5. *Servants think of ministry as an opportunity, not an obligation.* It doesn't matter what your age is. God will use you if you will begin to act and think like a servant."

Chapter 35. "God's Power in Your Weakness: God loves to use weak people...God will use us if we allow Him to work through our weaknesses. For that to happen, we must follow the model of Paul (the Apostle).

- *Admit your weaknesses.* Own up to your imperfections. Stop pretending to have it all together and be honest about yourself.

- *Be content with your weaknesses.* Your greatest life messages and your most effective ministry will come out of your deepest hurts. The things you're most embarrassed about, most ashamed of, and most reluctant to share are the very tools God can use most powerfully to heal others.
- *Honestly, share your weaknesses.* Humility is not putting yourself down or denying your strengths; rather, it is being honest about your weaknesses.
- *Glory in your weaknesses.* Instead of posing as self-confident and invincible, see yourself as a trophy of grace. When Satan points out your weaknesses, agree with him and fill your heart with praise for Jesus."

Part 6—You Were Made for a Mission

Chapter 36. "Made for a Mission: God is at work in the world, and He wants you to join Him. This assignment is called your *mission.* God wants you to have both a ministry in the Body of Christ and a mission in the world. Your ministry is your service to *believers*, and your mission is your service to *unbelievers.* Fulfilling your mission in the world is God's fifth purpose for your life.

Fulfilling your life mission on earth is an essential part of living for God's glory. The Bible gives several reasons why your mission is so important.

- *Your mission is a continuation of Jesus' mission on earth.* Jesus calls us not only to come to Him but to *go* for Him.
- *Your mission is a wonderful privilege.* Your mission involves two great privileges: working with God and representing Him.

- *Telling others how they can have eternal life is the greatest thing you can do for them.* We have the greatest news in the world, and sharing it is the greatest kindness you can show to anyone.
- *Your mission has eternal significance.* God wants you to share the Good News where you are…you should continually look for people God places in your path with whom you can share the gospel.
- *Your mission gives your life meaning.* If you fail to fulfill your God-given mission on earth, you will have wasted the life God gave you.
- *God's timetable for history's conclusion is connected to the completion of our commission.* What we *do* know for sure is this: Jesus will not return until everyone God wants to hear the Good News has heard it."

Chapter 37. "Sharing Your Life Message: God has given you a Life Message to share. When you became a believer, you also became God's messenger. God wants to speak to the world through you. Your Life Message has four parts to it:

1. Your *testimony:* the story of how you began a relationship with Jesus
2. Your *life lessons:* the most important lessons God has taught you
3. Your *godly passions:* the issues God shaped you to care about most
4. The *Good News:* the message of salvation."

Chapter 38. "Becoming a World-Class Christian: You have a choice to make. You will be either a *world-class* Christian or a *worldly* Christian. Worldly Christians look to God primarily for personal fulfillment. They are saved but self-centered. In contrast, world-class Christians know they were saved to serve and made for a mission. They are eager to receive a personal assignment and excited about the privilege of being used by God. World-class Christians are the only *fully alive* people on the planet.

How To Think Like a World-Class Christian

a. *Shift from self-centered thinking to other-centered thinking.* Think of the spiritual needs of unbelievers whenever you talk to them.

b. *Shift from local thinking to global thinking.* The first way to start thinking globally is to begin praying for specific countries. World-class Christians pray for the world.

c. *Shift from "here and now" thinking to eternal thinking.* To make the most of your time on earth, you must maintain an eternal perspective.

d. *Shift from thinking of excuses to thinking of creative ways to fulfill your commission.* God doesn't want to use just *some* of His people; He wants to use *all* of His people.

We are called to be *on a mission* for God. He wants His whole Church to take the whole gospel to the whole world."

Chapter 39. "Balancing Your Life: Your life is a pentathlon of five purposes, which you must keep in balance…they are summarized in the Great Commandment and the Great Commission of Jesus. These two statements sum up what this book is all about—God's five purposes for your life:

1. *'Love God with all your heart':* You were planned for God's pleasure, so your purpose is to love God through *worship.*

2. *'Love your neighbor as yourself':* You were shaped

for serving, so your purpose is to show love for others through *ministry.*

3. *'Go and make disciples':* You were made for a mission, so your purpose is to share God's message through *evangelism.*
4. *'baptize them into...':* You were formed for God's family, so your purpose is to identify with His church through *fellowship.*
5. *'teach them to do all things...':* You were created to become like Christ, so your purpose is to grow to maturity through *discipleship.*

A great commitment to the Great Commandment and the Great Commission will make you a great Christian.

This is what purpose-driven living is all about. Regardless of your age, the rest of your life can be the best of your life, and you can start living on purpose today."

Chapter 40. "Living with Purpose: Living on purpose is the only way to *really* live. Everything else is just existing. Most people struggle with three basic issues in life. The first is *identity:* 'Who am I?' The second is *importance:* 'Do I matter?' The third is *impact:* 'What is my place in life?' The answers to all three questions are found in God's five purposes for you, your *purpose statement*.

It's easy to drift away from what matters most and slowly get off course. To prevent this, you should develop a purpose statement for your life and then review it regularly.

- It's a statement that summarizes God's purpose for your life.
- It's a statement that points the direction of your life.
- It's a statement that defines 'success' for you.
- It's a statement that clarifies your roles.

- It's a statement that expresses your *SHAPE.*

Here are five questions you should consider as you prepare your *purpose statement*:

1. *What will be the center of my life?* This is the question of *worship.* Who are you going to live for? What are you going to build your life around?
2. *What will be the character of my life?* This is the question of *discipleship*. What kind of person will you be? God is far more interested in what you *are* than what you *do.*
3. *What will be the contribution of my life?* This is the question of *service.* What will be your ministry in the Body of Christ? Knowing your contribution of spiritual gifts, heart, abilities, personality, and experiences (SHAPE), what would be your best role in the family of God?
4. *What will be the communication of my life?* This is the question of your *mission* to unbelievers. It should include your commitment to share your testimony and the Good News with others.
5. *What will be the community of my life?* This is the question of *fellowship.* How will you demonstrate your commitment to other believers and connection to the family of God?

At the end of your life, it isn't going to matter at all what other people say about you. The only thing that will matter is *what God says* about you. Will you be a person God can use for his purposes? Will you serve God's purpose in *your* generation?"

PART 4:
Your Action Plans for a Successful Life Filled with Purpose, Peace & Prosperity

Before we begin looking at the final nuggets of wisdom for developing *Your Action Plans for a Successful Life Filled with Purpose, Peace, and Prosperity*, I'd like to leave you with one more bit of humor that had me laughing so hard I couldn't breathe. That's probably because I've been there, done that, got the T-shirt!

Preparing for a Colonoscopy

This Dave Barry column was originally published Feb. 22, 2008:

"I called my friend Andy Sable, a gastroenterologist, to make an appointment for a colonoscopy. A few days later, in his office, Andy showed me a color diagram of the colon, a lengthy organ that appears to go all over the place, at one point passing briefly through Minneapolis. Then Andy explained the colonoscopy procedure to me in a thorough, reassuring, and patient manner. I nodded thoughtfully, but I didn't really hear anything he said because my brain was shrieking, quote, 'HE'S GOING TO STICK A TUBE 17,000 FEET UP YOUR BUTT!'

I left Andy's office with some written instructions and a prescription for a product called 'MoviPrep,' which comes in a box large enough to hold a microwave oven. I will discuss MoviPrep in detail later; for now, suffice it to say that we must never allow it to fall into the hands of America's enemies.

I spent the next several days productively sitting around, being nervous. Then, on the day before my colonoscopy, I began my preparation. In accordance with my instructions, I didn't eat any solid food that day; all I had was chicken broth, which is basically water, only with less flavor. Then, in the evening, I took the MoviPrep. You mix two packets of powder together in a one-liter plastic jug, then you fill it with lukewarm water. (For those unfamiliar with the metric system, a liter is about 32 gallons.) Then you have to drink the whole jug. This takes about an hour because MoviPrep tastes—and here I am being kind—like a mixture of goat spit and urinal cleanser, with just a hint of lemon.

The instructions for MoviPrep, clearly written by somebody with a great sense of humor, state that after you drink it, 'a loose, watery bowel movement may result.'

This is kind of like saying that after you jump off your roof, you may experience contact with the ground.

MoviPrep is a nuclear laxative. I don't want to be too graphic here, but have you ever seen a space shuttle launch? This is pretty much the MoviPrep experience, with you as the shuttle. There are times when you wish the commode had a seat belt. You spend several hours pretty much confined to the bathroom, spurting violently. You eliminate *everything*. And then, when you figure you must be totally empty, you have to drink *another* liter of MoviPrep, at which point, as far as I can tell, your bowels travel into the future and start eliminating food that you have not even *eaten* yet.

After an action-packed evening, I finally got to sleep. The next morning, my wife drove me to the clinic. I was very nervous. Not only was I worried about the procedure, but I had been experiencing occasional return bouts of MoviPrep spurtage. I was thinking, 'What if I spurt on Andy?' How do you apologize to a friend for something like that? Flowers would not be enough.

At the clinic, I had to sign many forms acknowledging that I understood and totally agreed with whatever the heck the forms said. Then they led me to a room full of other colonoscopy people, where I went inside a little curtained space and took off my clothes and put on one of those hospital garments designed by sadist perverts, the kind that, when you put it on, makes you feel even more naked than when you are actually naked.

Then, a nurse named Eddie put a little needle in a vein

in my left hand. Ordinarily, I would have fainted, but Eddie was very good, and I was already lying down. Eddie also told me that some people put vodka in their MoviPrep. At first, I was ticked off that I hadn't thought of this, but then I pondered what would happen if you got yourself too tipsy to make it to the bathroom, so you were staggering around in full Fire Hose Mode. You would have no choice but to burn your house.

When everything was ready, Eddie wheeled me into the procedure room, where Andy was waiting with a nurse and an anesthesiologist. I did not see the 17,000-foot tube, but I knew Andy had it hidden around there somewhere. I was seriously nervous at this point.

Andy had me roll over on my left side, and the anesthesiologist began hooking something up to the needle in my hand. There was music playing in the room, and I realized that the song was *Dancing Queen* by Abba. I remarked to Andy that, of all the songs that could be playing during this particular procedure, *Dancing Queen* has to be the least appropriate.

'You want me to turn it up?' said Andy from somewhere behind me. 'Ha ha,' I said.

And then it was time, the moment I had been dreading for more than a decade. If you are squeamish, prepare yourself because I am going to tell you, in explicit detail, exactly what it was like.

I have no idea. Really. I slept through it. One moment, Abba was shrieking, 'Dancing Queen! Feel the beat from the tambourine…'

…and the next moment, I was back in the other room, waking up in a very mellow mood. Andy was looking down at me and asking me how I felt. I felt excellent. I felt even more excellent when Andy told me that it was all over and that my colon had passed with flying colors. I have never been prouder of an internal organ."

CHAPTER 19:
"17 Inches"—A GREAT Life Lesson!

Since we have grandsons who played baseball, this story quickly caught my attention. I soon realized it wasn't really about baseball at all but about life in general and how we choose to live it.

Also, please share this story with your family and friends, children and grandchildren, anyone you know in a leadership position, and any coaches you may know, regardless of the sport they coach.

By Ken Koenen | December 26, 2017

Twenty years ago, in Nashville, Tennessee, during the first week of January 1996, more than 4,000 baseball coaches descended upon the Opryland Hotel for the 52nd annual ABCA's (American Baseball Coaches Association) convention.

While I waited in line to register with the hotel staff, I heard other veteran coaches rumbling about the lineup of speakers scheduled to present during the weekend. One name kept resurfacing, always with the same sentiment—"John Scolinos is here? Oh, man, worth every penny of my airfare."

Who is John Scolinos, I wondered. No matter; I was just happy to be there.

In 1996, Coach Scolinos was 78 years old and five years retired from a college coaching career that began in 1948. He shuffled to the stage to an impressive standing ovation, wearing dark polyester pants, a light blue shirt, and a string around his neck from which home plate hung— a full-sized, stark-white home plate.

Seriously, I wondered, who is this guy?

After speaking for twenty-five minutes, not once mentioning the prop hanging around his neck, Coach Scolinos appeared to notice the snickering among some of the coaches.

Even those who knew Coach Scolinos had to wonder exactly where he was going with this or if he had simply forgotten about home plate since he'd gotten on stage. Then, finally …

"You're probably all wondering why I'm wearing a home plate around my neck," he said, his voice growing irascible. I laughed along with the others, acknowledging the possibility. "I may be old, but I'm not crazy. The reason I stand before you today is to share with you baseball people what I've learned in my life, what I've learned about home plate in my 78 years."

Several hands went up when Scolinos asked how many Little League coaches were in the room. "Do you know how wide home plate is in Little League?"

After a pause, someone offered, "Seventeen inches?" more of a question than an answer.

"That's right," he said. "How about in Babe Ruth's day? Any Babe Ruth coaches in the house?" Another long pause.

"Seventeen inches?" a guess from another reluctant coach.

"That's right," said Scolinos. "Now, how many high school coaches do we have in the room?" Hundreds of hands shot up as the pattern began to appear. "How wide is home plate in high school baseball?"

"Seventeen inches," they said, sounding more confident.

"You're right!" Scolinos barked. "And you college coaches, how wide is home plate in college?"

"Seventeen inches!" we said in unison.

"Any Minor League coaches here? How wide is home plate in pro ball?" "Seventeen inches!"

"RIGHT! And in the Major Leagues, how wide is home plate in the Major Leagues?

"Seventeen inches!"

"SEV-EN-TEEN INCHES!" he confirmed, his voice bellowing off the walls. "And what do they do with a Big-League pitcher who can't throw the ball over seventeen inches?" Pause. "They send him to Pocatello!" he hollered, drawing raucous laughter. "What they don't do is this: they don't say, 'Ah, that's okay, Jimmy. If you can't hit a seventeen-inch target, we'll make it eighteen inches or nineteen inches. We'll make it twenty inches so you have a better chance of hitting it. If you can't hit that, let us know so we can make it wider still, say twenty-five inches.'"

Pause. "Coaches… what do we do when your best player shows up late to practice? Or when our team rules forbid facial hair, and a guy shows up unshaven? What if he gets caught drinking? Do we hold him accountable? Or do we change the rules to fit him? Do we widen home plate? "

The chuckles gradually faded as four thousand coaches grew quiet, the fog lifting as the old coach's message began to unfold. He turned the plate toward himself and, using a Sharpie, began to draw something. When he turned it toward the crowd point up, a house was revealed, complete with a freshly drawn door and two windows. "This is the problem in our homes today. With our marriages, with the way we parent our kids. With our discipline.

We don't teach accountability to our kids, and there is no consequence for failing to meet standards. We just widen the plate!"

Pause. Then, to the point at the top of the house, he added a small American flag. "This is the problem in our schools today. The quality of our education is going downhill fast, and teachers have been stripped of the tools they need to be successful and to educate and discipline our young people. We are allowing others to widen home plate! Where is that getting us?"

Silence. He replaced the flag with a Cross. "And this is the problem in the Church, where powerful people in positions of authority have taken advantage of young children, only to have such an atrocity swept under the rug for years. Our church leaders are widening their home plate for themselves! And we allow it."

"And the same is true with our government. Our so-called representatives make rules for us that don't apply to themselves. They take bribes from lobbyists and foreign countries. They no longer serve us. And we allow them to widen home plate! We see our country falling into a dark abyss while we just watch."

I was amazed. At a baseball convention where I expected to learn something about curve balls and bunting and how to run better practices, I learned something far more valuable.

From an old man with a home plate strung around his neck, I had learned something about life, about myself, about my own weaknesses, and about my responsibilities as a leader.

I had to hold myself and others accountable to that which I knew to be right, lest our families, our faith, and our society continue down an undesirable path.

"If I am lucky," Coach Scolinos concluded, "you will remember one thing from this old coach today. It is this: "If we fail to hold ourselves to a higher standard, a standard of what we know to be right; if we fail to hold our spouses and our children to the same standards, if we are unwilling or unable to provide a consequence when they do not meet the standard; and if our schools & churches & our government fail to hold themselves accountable to those they serve, there is but one thing to look forward to…"

With that, he held the home plate in front of his chest, turned it around, and revealed its dark black backside, "...We have dark days ahead!"

Note: Coach Scolinos died in 2009 at the age of 91, but not before touching the lives of hundreds of players and coaches, including mine. Meeting him at my first ABCA convention kept me returning year after year, looking for similar wisdom and inspiration from other coaches. He is the best clinic speaker the ABCA has ever known because he was so much more than a baseball coach. His message was clear: "Coaches, keep your players—no matter how good they are—your own children, your churches, your government, and most of all, keep yourself at seventeen inches."

And this, my friends, is what our country has become and what is wrong with it today, and now go out there and fix it! "Don't widen the plate."

CHAPTER 20: Beating the Competition in Your Next Job Interview

Many job seekers are under the false impression that a slick resume is the key to securing that job they so badly want. It's true your resume should be as attractive, truthful, and concise as possible without boring readers with a lot of unnecessary details.

However, make no mistake: your resume is just a tool designed to ignite enough interest to get your foot in the door for that all-important *job interview.*

The interview process is where you must be ready to effectively sell yourself and put yourself in a position at the head of all the rest of your job-seeking competitors. The only way to do that is *preparation, preparation, preparation!*

I must confess I didn't fully understand how important preparation for a job interview was and what it meant to properly prepare for an interview until I was preparing to interview for my last job at the age of 64! I firmly believe my preparation for that interview made all the difference in helping me rise above the rest of the pack competing for that job.

In fact, and in retrospect, I realize now that I probably knocked myself out of several great job opportunities because I was not properly prepared for the interview process.

So, what changed in my ability to properly prepare for a job interview? I ran across Dan Miller's website, 48Days.com, and ordered his book, *48 Days To The Work You Love.*

Everything Miller wrote about in that book made so much sense to me that I committed to putting it into practice when I decided to be a candidate for that last job I spoke of earlier at the age of 64!

It made me realize that you're never too old to compete for a job opportunity if you possess the skills and experience for that position and, most importantly, if you are properly prepared for the interview process.

I'm going to share some nuggets of wisdom from Dan Miller's book, *48 Days to the Work You Love,* hoping you, too, will find his wisdom as valuable as I did and want to learn more before seeking your next job opportunity.

Proper Preparation for a Job Interview

Dan Miller says, "The keys to successful interviewing are preparation, knowing what to expect, and practice.

Preparation is the single most important factor in successful interviews. Your preparation should involve *two primary components: knowing yourself and knowing the company.*"

Knowing Yourself

Miller states, "Critical to presenting yourself well and securing a position that will be meaningful and fulfilling is the process of self-assessment. You should be intimately familiar with your (1) skills and abilities, (2) personality tendencies, and (3) values, dreams, and passions.

Be prepared in this regard to answer the following questions in the interview (…these few are critical in thoroughly knowing yourself):

Tell me a little about yourself. This is a standard question in almost every interview. In some ways, it is probably the most important question in your interview, and you *must* prepare your answer well in advance."

I confess again that I didn't understand how important this question was, and I know I lost out on at least one job opportunity I was really interested in! I would actually get angry when asked this question. I thought it was so stupid since the interviewers had my resume and could find out as much as they wanted to know about me! I totally didn't get it!

Miller goes on to say, "The interviewer will expect you to have developed an answer for this question, and if you have not, you will appear ill-prepared, and the interview will be off to a very poor start.

Remember, your answer to any question should be no more than *2 minutes* in length. On this particular one, you might spend 15 seconds on your personal background, 1 minute on your career highlights, a few seconds on your strongest professional achievements, and then conclude by explaining why you are looking for a new opportunity.

Ask yourself, 'What can I contribute to this company?' and let that guide your response. Regardless of the content of your answer, you should outline the answer to this question on paper and then practice it many times until you can repeat it concisely.

What are 3 of your strengths? If you cannot clearly identify and describe your strengths, how do you expect an interviewer to pull them out in the brief encounter of an interview?

Tell me about a weakness and what you have done to work on it. Don't play ignorant or modestly claim perfection. Be prepared to talk about something you struggle with. At the same time, stay positive regarding what you have done to improve.

What skills do you possess that have prepared you for this job? Obviously, you need to have researched the company and the job, or you will be unprepared for this question.

What are your short and long-term goals? Talk about personal goals as well as business goals. Companies today are looking for balanced individuals who are interested in things other than work."

In his book, Dan Miller offers 21 questions you may be asked by an interviewer, questions you need to have a 1-to-2-minute answer prepared in advance.

I had a well-thought-out, honest answer for every one of those 21 questions and reviewed them over and over again until I was confident I could answer any or all of them when asked.

The following are the 21 questions Miller suggests you should have a pre-planned honest answer to:

1. “Tell me a little about yourself.
2. What are your greatest strengths? What are three characteristics that would make you a good candidate for this position?
3. What would your previous employer list as your greatest strengths?
4. What motivates you to put forth your greatest effort?
5. What have been some of your most significant accomplishments? How were you able to achieve those accomplishments?
6. What have you done that has contributed to increased sales, profits, efficiency, etc?
7. What types of situations frustrate you? What are your weaknesses? What have you attempted and failed to accomplish?
8. What are you looking for in a new position? Why do you want this job? What do you find attractive about this position?
9. Why are you leaving your current job?
10. What important changes or trends do you see in this industry? How do you think those changes will affect the way we succeed in this company?

11. How long will it take you to make a meaningful contribution to our company? What are the areas in which you would need more training? Do you feel you may be overqualified or too experienced for this position?
12. What do you look for in a supervisor? Describe the relationship that should exist between a supervisor and his/her employee. What do you see as your most difficult task as a manager? What is your management style?
13. Do you prefer working alone or as part of a team? Are you better working with things, people, or ideas? Are you better at creating or doing?
14. Describe an ideal working environment. In your last position, what were the things you liked most and least? How do you handle pressure and deadlines?
15. Where on your list of priorities does your job fall? What kind of things outside of work do you enjoy? What magazines do you like to read? Name three books you have read in the last years. Are you achieving personal goals you have set?
16. Where would you like to be 5 years from now? What would you expect to be earning 5 years from now? Are you continuing your education? How are you staying current with changes in this industry?
17. How long do you feel a person should stay in the same position?
18. What does a typical weekend consist of for you? What do you do to relieve boredom?
19. What other kinds of positions have you been looking at? If we do not select you for this position, would you be interested in another position with this company? How does this job compare with others for

which you have interviewed? What makes this job different from your current or last one?

20. Why should we choose you for this position? What can you do for us that someone else cannot do?
21. Do you have any questions? (A good interviewer will ask you this.)"

Knowing the Company

Miller states, "Knowledge of the company or organization, its products and services, its standing in the community, and the key individuals involved is essential.

In addition, you should obtain information about the company's annual growth rate, annual sales, number of employees, location of the company headquarters, and its major changes such as buyouts or mergers and industry trends.

The information you have, which will lead to questions you can ask, can easily tip the scales in your favor during the interview.

Make sure you are ready with 4 to 5 questions. Even if the interviewer has answered everything you need to know, it will make you appear more interested and more knowledgeable if you ask a few questions."

It's a process well worth committing to if you want to shine above the competition. It may seem like a daunting task at first, but it will help you really take a serious assessment of yourself in a number of very beneficial ways.

Miller also offers the following 21 questions you can choose from to ask the interviewer:

1. "What would be a typical day's assignments?
2. What are the travel requirements, if any?
3. What is the typical career path in this position? What is a realistic time frame for advancement?

4. Where are the opportunities for greatest growth within the company?
5. What criteria are used to evaluate and promote employees here?
6. What type of training is available?
7. What kind of ongoing professional development programs are available to help me continue to grow?
8. Whom would I report to in this position? What can you tell me about that person's management style?
9. What management philosophy is used by the company?
10. How would you describe the company's culture (personality, environment)?
11. What is the company's mission statement? What are the company's goals?
12. What are the skills and attributes most needed to advance in this company?
13. Who will be this company's major competitors over the next five years? How will this company maintain an advantage over them?
14. What has been the growth pattern of this company over the last five years?
15. What do you see as upcoming changes in this industry?
16. Is this a new position, or would I be replacing someone?
17. What qualities are you looking for in the right person for this position?
18. Is there a written job description? May I see it?
19. How many people are in this department?
20. How do you see me complementing the existing group?
21. What do you enjoy about working for this company?"

I can honestly attest to the fact that *48 Days To The Work You Love* totally prepared me with the information and confidence I needed to shine above my competition at the age of 64 and win that job doing the work I knew I would love!

A very important part of job-seeking is to have a vision for what you want your future to look like and then develop a plan to make your vision a reality.

You've probably heard it said, "You have to plan your work and then work your plan."

The next chapter will help you with this process.

CHAPTER 21:
(20) Building Blocks for Visioncasting and Planning Your Future

Proverbs 29:18 (NKJV) says, *"Where there is no revelation* (vision)*, the people cast off restraint* (perish)."

In other words, if we don't have a vision and have not planned a course of action for our lives from year to year, then we just tend to wander aimlessly through life, hoping great things will happen. Over time, the lack of vision and planning just tends to breed a great deal of frustration and disappointment that often leads to discouragement!

In this chapter, I'll be sharing wisdom on visioncasting from Andy Stanley, the founding pastor of North Point Community Church in Atlanta, GA. His book, *Visioneering,* was a life-changing resource for me. I only wish I had read it thirty years ago! However, the wisdom he presents can and should be applied on a regular basis regardless of your age and vocation.

Stanley writes, "Everybody ends up somewhere in life. You can end up somewhere on purpose."

He defines *visioneering* as "the engineering of a vision. It's the process one follows to develop and maintain vision. Vision is a clear mental picture of what *could be*, fueled by the conviction that it *should be."*

He writes, "Vision is a preferred future. A destination. Vision always stands in contrast to the world as it is. Vision demands change. It implies movement."

Stanley continues, "Without vision, chances are you will come to the end of your life and wonder. Wonder what you could have done—what you should have done. And like so many, you may wonder if your life really mattered at all."

Whether you believe in the Bible or not, whether you

believe in God or not, I know you will take away some great wisdom from what Stanley has to say about vision.

1. *"A Vision Begins As a Concern:* Something will bother you about the way things are or the way things are headed."
2. *"A Vision Does Not Necessarily Require Immediate Action:* Developing or discovering a vision for a particular area of our lives takes time. It always requires patience."
3. *"Pray for Opportunities and Plan as If You Expect God to Answer Your Prayers:* Praying and planning will help you keep your vision alive. Pray for the people who could help you launch your vision. And while you wait, plan! Develop a strategy. Dream on paper. Find the one or two things you *can* do and get busy."
4. *"God Is Using Your Circumstances to Position and Prepare You to Accomplish His Vision for Your Life:* Often, there is no tangible connection between our circumstances and the vision God has given us. He desires to work through your circumstances to maneuver you into proper position."
5. *"What God Originates, He Orchestrates:* How is never a problem for God. It is usually a big problem for us. But *how* is God's specialty."
6. *"Walk Before You Talk; Investigate Before You Initiate:* To share a vision prematurely usually guarantees a less than warm reception. There is usually some background work that needs to be done before you go public with your idea."
7. *"Communicate Your Vision As a Solution to a Problem That Must Be Addressed Immediately:* Vision-casting will always include an element of waking people out of their apathy.

8. *"Cast Your Vision to the Appropriate People at the Appropriate Time:* A carefully crafted vision has the ability to capture people's imaginations as well as their commitment. People will reprioritize their lives and lifestyles in order to be part of a vision they feel called to."
9. *"Don't Expect Others to Take Greater Risks or Make Greater Sacrifices Than You Have:* There is something inauthentic about a man or woman who casts a vision for which he or she is not willing to personally sacrifice. It is hypocritical to ask others to take risks we are not willing to take ourselves."
10. *"Don't Confuse Your Plans with God's Vision:* When we lose sight of the distinction between our plans and the vision we are pursuing, we set ourselves up for a large dose of discouragement. Failed plans should not be interpreted as a failed vision."
11. *"Visions Are Refined—They Don't Change; Plans Are Revised—They Rarely Stay the Same:* Be stubborn about the vision. Be flexible with your plans. Strategies and timelines are always up for grabs."
12. *"Respond to Criticism with Prayer, Remembrance, and If Necessary, a Revision of the Plan:* Don't be afraid to learn from your critics."
13. *"Visions Thrive in an Environment of Unity; They Die in an Environment of Division:* It is okay to have problems. It is not okay to ignore them.
14. *"Abandon the Vision Before You Abandon Your Moral Authority:* Maintain your moral authority at all costs. As a visionary, it is your primary point of leverage. Without it, you are no longer a leader worth following."
15. *"Don't Get Distracted:* You don't want to wake up

one day and realize you have *spent* your time rather than *invested* it."

16. *"There Is Divine Potential in All You Envision to Do:* The truth is, our secular pursuits have more kingdom potential than our religious ones. For it is in the realm of our secular pursuits that secular people are watching."
17. *"The End of a God-Ordained Vision Is God:* When God shows up, everybody in the vicinity is affected. Believers, unbelievers, committed, uncommitted, it doesn't matter. The power of His presence in even small doses will leave its mark."
18. *"Maintaining a Vision Requires Adherence to a Set of Core Beliefs and Behaviors:* To keep a vision moving in the right direction, those involved must embrace a mutually agreed-upon code of conduct."
19. *"Visions Require Constant Attention:* As a leader, it is essential that your decisions be anchored to your vision."
20. *"Maintaining a Vision Requires Bold Leadership:* Don't be afraid to hold people accountable to previously agreed-upon standards. Don't tolerate those things that have the potential to derail your vision. Deal with them."

CHAPTER 22:
The Value and Power of Setting Goals

According to Dan Miller, author of *48 Days to the Work You Love*, "there is considerable evidence to indicate that expectations of your future do, in fact, tend to create your future. People usually end up pretty much where they expect.

It seems reasonable, then, to spend some time determining specific, worthwhile expectations that will make your life more meaningful. If you don't have a written plan for your life, it may feel like you're driving a car without having your hands on the wheel.

Are you a goal-setter? Do you typically set goals at the first of the year? If not, why not?

Goals are not written in concrete and unchangeable terms, but they do give you a starting point and a destination. The important thing is that you are in charge when working on your goals. It is the easiest way to put yourself in the driver's seat of your life.

Your life has meaning only when you are working toward goals that you have decided on.

In order for your purpose in life to be fulfilled, you must set goals in multiple areas. Success is not just career or financial—family, physical, and spiritual are equally important areas of achievement. They are part of the same whole, balanced person.

Any stage in life can be an exciting time with many opportunities or a dreary time of confusion and entrapment. You may not be able to change your circumstances, but you can decide that the circumstances won't dominate you. You do have choices.

There is something magical that happens when you write down your goals.

Here's the framework for this entire process.

- If we were meeting three years from today, what has to have happened during that three-year period for you to feel happy about your progress?
- What are the biggest dangers you'll have to face and deal with in order to achieve that progress?
- What are the biggest opportunities you have that you would need to focus on and capture to achieve those things?
- What strengths will you need to reinforce and maximize, and what skills and resources will you need to develop that you don't currently have in order to capture those opportunities?

Begin with the three-year goals and then work backward to what you need to do today to make deposits in what you want your life to be three years from now. Be specific, creating quantifiable benchmarks to track your deposits of success."

Dan Miller believes, "The best way to predict your future is to create it."

Your Personal Goal Planning Guide

Dan Miller asks, "If nothing changed in your life over the next 3 years, would that be okay?" You can use his detailed guide for visioncasting and goal setting in what Miller calls *"the 7 main aspects of life."*

To download a free copy of Dan Miller's Goal Planning Guide, please go to my website at www.wisdom-matters.com, click on the "Free Resources" tab, go to the last resource entitled "Goal Planning Guide," and click on it to view the guide. You will notice that the guide is entitled "2020-Goals-Workbook." Click on the 3 dots (…) on the top right-hand side of the page, then click on "Download This File."

Don't be confused by the fact that the guide says, "My Goals for 2020 and Beyond." This guide can be used no matter what year(s) you are planning for.

You are never too old to set another goal or dream a new dream!

CHAPTER 23:
Your Life Conversion Guide to Eternal Peace and Happiness

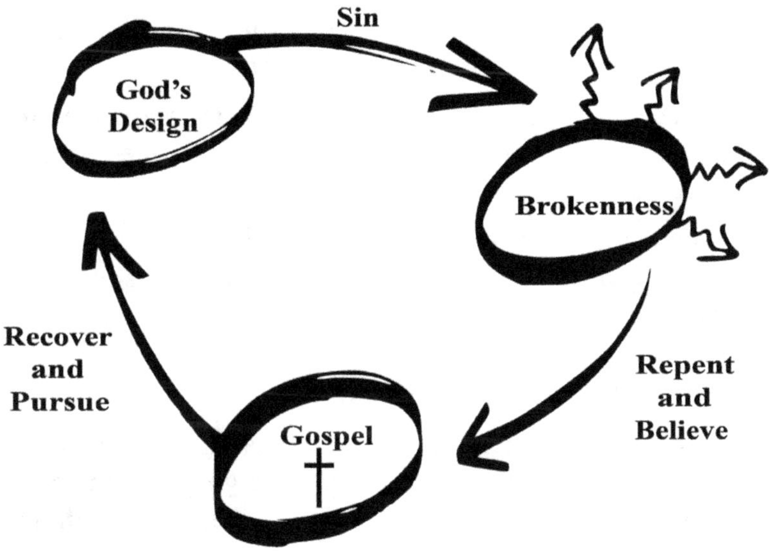

God's Design

The Bible tells us that God has a design for our lives and that He cares for every aspect of our lives. That includes our choices, our finances, our relationships—everything. If we live according to God's design, then we can live under God's blessing. The problem is that all of us tend to depart from God's design.

Sin

The Bible has a word for when we depart from God's design, reject His counsel, and try to live life on our own terms—that word is "sin." And when we sin—when we leave His design—we land in a place of brokenness.

Brokenness

We see brokenness all around us—just read today's headlines. If we're honest, we also see it in our own lives. It looks like broken relationships, addiction, depression, guilt, shame, and regret. And we always try to fix it, don't we? We try a different relationship, a different job, a drug of some sort, or maybe we try to be more religious.

Whatever we do, we are trying to fix or escape the brokenness. But brokenness is not a bad thing. In fact, it helps us understand that we need change in our lives.

The bad news is the change we need cannot come from within ourselves. The good news is the Bible tells us where the change we need comes from.

The Gospel (God's Good News)

The change we need comes from what the Bible calls the gospel, which means "good news." The gospel is the story of Jesus. Jesus is the Son of God, who came to earth and never departed from God's design. The Bible says He lived a perfect, sinless life. But Jesus was crucified on the cross.

The Bible says Jesus died on the cross "for the sins of the world." That includes mine and yours. When Jesus was on the cross, God put the sins of the world—mine, yours, everyone who has ever lived or will ever live—on Jesus.

And Jesus received the punishment for those sins, which the Bible says is death. After He died, He was buried but rose from the dead three days later. The Bible says Jesus was raised from the dead to prove that He was who He said He was—the Son of God who can forgive our sins because He paid the price for them. When He forgives sin, He heals the broken places in our lives.

Repent and Believe

But just hearing it is not enough. We must act on it by admitting our sinful brokenness. We must ask God to forgive us. We do this by turning away from sin and trusting in Jesus. This is what it means to repent and believe.

Repent means to change our minds and change our direction by believing in the gospel story that Jesus was crucified for our sins and was raised from the dead. When we believe, we receive new life through Jesus. The Bible says that when we repent and believe, God will send His Holy Spirit into our lives, forgive our sins, and begin to heal our inner brokenness.

Recover and Pursue

When we repent and believe, God gives us the opportunity to recover from our brokenness and pursue His design for our lives. The best part is that He lets us do that from wherever we are. There's no need to go back and fix anything. It's not necessary to "get better first." We can start recovering from our brokenness and pursuing that perfect design from where we are right now.

Now that you have heard this good news, and if you sincerely believe it, God wants you to respond to Him. Are you ready to take action, to take the next step that can change your life forever?

You can talk to Him using words like these:

- God, my life is broken, and I recognize it's because of my sins. I need You.
- I believe Jesus came to live and to die and was raised from the dead to rescue me from my sins.
- Forgive me, God. I want to turn from my selfish, sinful ways and put my faith and trust in You.

- I now believe Jesus is my Savior and Lord of all. Fill me with Your Holy Spirit to empower and strengthen me to follow Jesus from this day forward.

If you sincerely believe with all your heart, soul, mind, and strength what you have just read in this chapter, and you have surrendered your life to Jesus, you are now a child of God empowered by His Holy Spirit to begin a new life filled with hope for a brighter future filled with purpose, peace, and prosperity, both now and for eternity.

CONCLUSION: It's Time for ACTION

The first step in getting somewhere IS TO DECIDE that you are not going to stay where you are. —Author Unknown

Denzel Washington's "Three Simple Rules in Life":

1. If you don't go after what you want, *you'll never have it.*
2. If you don't ask, *the answer is always NO.*
3. If you don't step forward, *you're always in the same place.*

Do you know what the definition of "insanity" is? It's doing the same things over and over again, expecting different results.

If you are at a point right now, no matter your age, where you feel like you are in a rut or feel like you have no real purpose or direction in life, the only way you can change that and move from where you are today to where you'd like to be, is to *TAKE ACTION!*

If you are serious about making some positive changes in your life, I firmly believe the wisdom and tools in this book, if committed to and acted upon, will put you on a new path and take you to that new place in life you've only been dreaming about until now.

Remember, dreams and visions without a plan to *TAKE ACTION* are only time-wasting daydreams that will never change a thing, especially you!

Here's the BIG SECRET. For life transformation to become real and meaningful and to last a lifetime, you will need supernatural power, a power far greater than your own.

You may not be ready to hear this right now, but I am a living testimony to what that "supernatural power" can do. The only way to receive that kind of power is to reread Chapter 23 and *TAKE ACTION!*

My sincere prayer is that you will accept my challenge to reread Chapter 23 and see if the Almighty Sovereign God of all creation will open your eyes, your heart, and your mind with a burning desire to walk with Him from this day forward. If not, don't worry. His timing is perfect.

Ultimately, it's still your choice. Keep doing the same things you've been doing, expecting different results (the definition of insanity), or *TAKE ACTION* now to begin experiencing your God-blessed new life.

THE TOP LINE and THE BOTTOM LINE:

"You can't go back and change the beginning, but you can start where you are and change the ending."

If you change nothing…Nothing will change!

BIBLIOGRAPHY

Part 1—Personal Growth & Leadership Wisdom

Chapter 1: Attitude Is Everything, John Maxwell, *The Winning Attitude*, (San Bernardino, CA: Here's Life Publishers, © 1991)

Chapter 2: What It Takes to Be a Winner, Jim Tressell, *The Winners Manual: For the Game of Life*, (Carol Stream, IL: Tyndale House Publishers, Copyright © 2008)

Chapter 3: Becoming the Person Others Will Follow, John Maxwell, *The 21 Indispensable Qualities Of A Leader*, (Nashville, TN: Thomas Nelson, Inc., Copyright, © 1999)

Chapter 4: Follow These Laws and People Will Follow You, John Maxwell, *The 21 Irrefutable Laws Of Leadership*, (Nashville, TN: Thomas Nelson, Inc., Copyright, © 1998)

Chapter 5: "Leadership vs Management: The Difference That Will Change the Way You Work," Lindsay Pietroluongo, *Elegant Themes*, Accessed June 20, 2024, https://www.elegantthemes.com/blog/business/leadership-vs-management-the-difference-that-will-change-the-way-you-work

Chapter 8: Problem-Solving Made Easy, Tim Hansel, *Eating Problems for Breakfast: A Creative Guide to Problem-Solving,* (Copyright 1988 by Tim Hansel)

Chapter 9: "7 Entrepreneurial Lessons From 'Shark Tank,'" Amber Mac, *Fast Company*, Accessed June 20, 2024, https://www.fastcompany.com/1826393/7-entrepreneurial-lessons-shark-tank

Chapter 10: Secrets to Success for Any Path You Choose in Life, Dale Carnegie, *How To Win Friends And Influ-*

ence People, (New York, NY: Simon and Schuster, Copyright 1936, copyright renewed © 1964, Revised Edition copyright © 1981)

Part 2—Financial Wisdom

Chapter 11: How to Become a Billionaire, Scot Anderson, *Think Like a Billionaire, Become A Billionaire—As A Man Thinks, So Is He* (Mesa, AZ: Winword Publishing, Inc., First Edition, Copyright © 2006)

Chapter 12: Get Out of Debt and Start Building Wealth, Larry Burkett, *How to Manage Your Money Workbook*, (© 1975, 1982, 1991, 2000, Revised Edition 2000)

Chapter 14: DEBT – The Good, the Bad, and the Ugly, David Bach, *The Finish Rich Workbook*, (New York, NY: Broadway Books, a division of Random House, First Edition, Copyright © 2003)

Part 3—Spiritual Wisdom

Chapter 16: The Wisest Person the World Has Ever Known, *The Holy Bible, New International Version*, (Grand Rapids, MI: Zondervan, copyright © 1985 by Zondervan)

Chapter 17: Character-Building Wisdom, *Holy Bible, New Living Translation*, (Carol Stream, IL: Tyndale House Publishers, copyright © 1996)

Chapter 18: Living with Purpose and Peace, Rick Warren, *The Purpose Driven Life*. (Grand Rapids, MI: Zondervan, Copyright © 2002)

Part 4—Your Action Plans for a Successful Life Filled with Purpose, Peace & Prosperity

First section of Part 4: Preparing for a Colonoscopy, Dave Barry, February 22, 2008: https://www.miamiherald.com/living/liv-columns-blogs/dave-barry/article1928847.html

Chapter 19: "17 Inches" – A GREAT Life Lesson!, Ken Koenen, December 26, 2017: https://www.facebook.com/ken.koenen.5

Chapter 20: Beating the Competition in Your Next Job Interview, Dan Miller, *48 Days To The Work You Love*, (Nashville, TN: Broadman & Holman Publishers, © 2005)

Chapter 21: (20) Building Blocks for Visioncasting & Planning Your Future, Andy Stanley, *Visioneering*, (Sisters, OR: Multnomah Publishers, Inc., © 1999)

Chapter 22: The Value and Power of Setting Goals, Dan Miller, *48 Days To The Work You Love*, (Nashville, TN: Broadman & Holman Publishers, © 2005)

Chapter 23: Your Life Conversion Guide to Eternal Peace and Happiness, Jimmy Scroggins and Steve Wright, *Turning Everyday Conversations Into Gospel Conversations,* (Nashville, TN: B&H Publishing Group, Copyright © 2016 by Family Church)

ABOUT THE AUTHOR

Earl Runcan is an entrepreneur at heart who has owned and operated several businesses. He has also worked in the nonprofit sector as Executive Director of an inner-city medical clinic and a neighborhood revitalization ministry. Earl and his wife, Lynn, have two married daughters. Amy and Tim blessed them with two granddaughters, Abby and Saralyn. Carrie and Jeremy blessed them with two grandsons, Dylan and Ben. Earl has been a Ruling Elder in the Evangelical Presbyterian Church since 1991. He published his first book, *What IN the World Is Wrong with This World*, in 2018 and currently writes on his blog *Wisdom-Matters* at www.wisdom-matters.com.